P9-DGG-347

Daily Readings

—————— FROM ——————

YOU
CAN
YOU
WILL

Daily Readings

— FROM —

YOU
CAN
YOU
WILL

90 Devotions to
Becoming a **WINNER**

#1 *NEW YORK TIMES* BESTSELLING AUTHOR

JOEL OSTEEN

*Faith
Words*

New York • Boston • Nashville

Unless otherwise indicated, all Scripture quotations are taken from *The Holy Bible, New International Version*® NIV®. Copyright © 1973, 1978, 1984, 2011 by Biblica, Inc.™ Used by permission. All rights reserved worldwide.

Scripture quotations noted NLT are taken from the *Holy Bible, New Living Translation*, copyright © 1996, 2004, 2007 by Tyndale House Foundation. Used by permission of Tyndale House Publishers, Inc., Carol Stream, Illinois 60188. All rights reserved.

Scripture quotations noted NKJV are taken from the *New King James Version* of the Bible. Copyright © 1982 by Thomas Nelson, Inc. Used by permission. All rights reserved.

Scripture quotations noted AMP are from *The Amplified Bible*. Copyright © 1954, 1958, 1962, 1964, 1965, 1987 by The Lockman Foundation. All rights reserved. Used by permission. (www.Lockman.org)

Scripture quotations noted KJV are from the *King James Version* of the Holy Bible.

Scriptures noted MSG are from *The Message*. Copyright © 1993, 1994, 1995, 1996, 2000, 2001, 2002. Used by permission of NavPress Publishing Group.

Literary development and design: Koechel Peterson & Associates, Inc., Minneapolis, Minnesota.

This book has been adapted from *You Can, You Will*, copyright © 2014 by Joel Osteen. Published by FaithWords.

FaithWords
Hachette Book Group
1290 Avenue of the Americas
New York, NY 10104
www.faithwords.com

Printed in the United States of America

First Edition: October 2015
10 9 8 7 6 5 4 3 2 1

FaithWords is a division of Hachette Book Group, Inc. The FaithWords name and logo are trademarks of Hachette Book Group, Inc.

The Hachette Speakers Bureau provides a wide range of authors for speaking events. To find out more, go to www.hachettespeakersbureau.com or call (866) 376-6591.

The publisher is not responsible for websites (or their content) that are not owned by the publisher.

Library of Congress Cataloging-in-Publication Data: 2015935580

ISBN: 978-1-4555-6049-3

Contents

Introduction

Perhaps your life today is confusing, chaotic, messy, and the choices you face are baffling. If you are like most of us, as you are trying to make sense of your life, you're listening to people who try to squeeze you into their molds and pressure you into being who they want you to be. Too often we allow doubts, fears, and the discouraging things people have said to limit us and convince us to settle where we are. We look to them in hopes of finding some meaning and direction for our lives, and the answers we get prove to be empty and shallow. Far too many of us conclude that the best we can hope for is merely to make it through, to find a way to tough it out and make ends meet.

The truth is that there is a winner inside of you, but too often we talk ourselves out of God's best. You were created to be successful, to accomplish your goals, to leave your mark on this generation. You can bring the dreams of your heart to fulfillment and become the person you've always wanted to be. You have greatness in you. The key is to get it out.

That is why I wrote my book *You Can, You Will*, which provides eight undeniable qualities of a winner and the encouragement that will help you reach your potential so you can become all you were created to be. I've seen these qualities work in my own life and in the lives of many others:

1. *Create bold visions—Dare to dream big dreams.*

2. *Run your own race—Focus on your unique course and goals.*

3. *Think positively—Control your thoughts and attitudes.*

4. *Expect good things to happen—Anticipate great opportunities.*

5. *Stay passionate—Light the fire within and approach life with enthusiasm.*

6. *Commit to excellence—Do your best and maintain high standards.*

7. *Keep growing—Deal with your weaknesses and continually improve.*

8. *Serve others—Invest yourself in others.*

No matter where you are or what challenges you are facing, you have what it takes to win. You didn't get shortchanged. You're not lacking. You're fully equipped. You're talented enough. You're smart enough. You're experienced enough. You have the right personality and the right looks. You're the right nationality. You're the man or woman for the job.

This collection of ninety daily devotionals contains excerpts from my original book that emphasize positive, inspiring, and faith-building messages, along with additional supportive and encouraging material in the form of key Bible verses, daily prayers, and daily thoughts.

I hope my words and the other material in this daily devotional will lift your spirits, ignite your faith, and increase God's favor in your life.

Daily Readings from You Can, You Will is divided into eight sections. Each section covers one of the eight undeniable qualities of a winner. The goal is for you to take just a brief time each day to read and reflect, to put the events and circumstances in your life in perspective, and to receive a mental, emotional, and spiritual lift.

Each of the daily readings was selected to emphasize the undeniable qualities of a winner. I've added several other features to help you apply and live out the truth that God wants you to know. Therefore, each daily devotional includes:

A suggested Scripture reading: These passages will sometimes relate directly to the point being described, and in other instances the reading will provide necessary background for accurately understanding the truth for that day. Please don't neglect these brief selections from God's Word if you want to gain the full benefit of this book.

Key verse(s): A biblical verse or verses that specifically express the theme of the devotional.

A devotional excerpt from *You Can, You Will*: A brief story or lesson that I believe will encourage and uplift you.

Today's Prayer: A daily prayer that can serve as a model to help you express your prayer requests, desires, gratitude, and fresh commitments to God. Feel free to adapt these prayers and make them your own. Have a personal conversation with your heavenly Father.

Today's Thought: These are points meant for you to consider prayerfully after each daily reading. God's Word tells us that our thinking patterns become our acting patterns. The way we talk to ourselves greatly influences our actions. The Today's Thought sections are meant to encourage you to agree with *what God thinks of you* throughout each day.

These ninety readings should be read at a one-each-day pace so that they carry you through three months or so. As you put these principles on the eight qualities into action, you will step into a new level of your destiny. You will discover talents you didn't know you had, and you will see God's blessing and favor in amazing ways.

This is your moment!
YOU CAN!
YOU WILL!

Daily Readings

YOU CAN
YOU WILL

Keep YOUR VISION *in Front of* YOU

The Power of Visual Reminders

Scripture Reading: Genesis 50 (especially vv. 18–20)

When [Joseph] told his father as well as his brothers,
his father rebuked him and said, "What is this dream you had?
Will your mother and I and your brothers actually
come and bow down to the ground before you?"

Genesis 37:10

A young man dreamed of being an actor, but in the early 1980s, he wasn't getting the big parts he wanted. Broke and discouraged, he drove his beat-up old car to the top of a hill overlooking the city of Los Angeles and did something unusual. He wrote himself a check for ten million dollars for "Acting services rendered."

This young man had grown up so poor that his family lived in a Volkswagen van at one time. He put that check in his wallet and kept it there. When things got tough, he'd pull it out and look at it to remind himself of his dream. A dozen years later, that same young man, the comedian Jim Carrey, was making fifteen million to twenty-five million dollars a movie.

Studies tell us that we move toward what we consistently see. You should keep something in front of you, even if it's symbolic, to remind you of what you are believing for. For instance, I met a businessman who had a goal to build a new office for his company. He bought a brick, the same type of brick he wanted to use on his building. He keeps that brick on his desk. Every time he sees it, he's moving toward his goal. It reminds him of what he's dreaming about.

If you're single and you want to get married, put an empty photo album on your table. That's where you're going to put your wedding photos. When you see it, you're moving toward it.

You may not be reaching your highest potential, not because you don't have the faith, the talent, or the determination, but because you're not keeping the right things in front of you. All over your house, you should have pictures that inspire you, Scripture verses that encourage you, mementoes that strengthen your faith. Maybe one of them is a key on your key ring for the new house you want to buy.

TODAY'S PRAYER

Father, You put a dream in Joseph's heart, which You brought to pass despite one obstacle after another, and You've put a dream in my heart as well. I believe that this word is for me today and that as I am moving toward my goal, You are working to bring it to pass. Amen.

TODAY'S THOUGHT

Do not be afraid to dream lofty dreams.
We serve the Most High God, and nothing is too hard for Him. He makes the impossible possible!

God Will Finish What He Started

Scripture Reading: Zechariah 4

And I am convinced and sure of this very thing, that He Who began a good work in you will continue until the day of Jesus Christ [right up to the time of His return], developing [that good work] and perfecting and bringing it to full completion in you.

Philippians 1:6 AMP

In the Scriptures, Zerubbabel wanted to rebuild the temple. He laid the foundation, but then the people came against him and made him stop. For ten years no work was done. One day the prophet Zechariah told him to get the headstone, which was reserved to be the last piece of stone that went into the building. It was symbolic of the finished product.

Why was it important for Zerubbabel to keep the headstone in front of him? Because every time he looked at the headstone, it was a reminder that God would finish what He started. When Zerubbabel was discouraged and thought it was impossible to finish the job, he would look at the headstone. That was God saying to him, "I'm in control. I'm going to bring it to pass. Just stay in faith."

My brother-in-law Kevin is a twin. Growing up, his dream was to have twins. He and my sister Lisa tried to have a baby for a long time with no success. Lisa went through all the fertility treatments, including several surgeries, but still nothing. They were very discouraged; it didn't look like it would ever happen. Then one day there was a package from Huggies in their mailbox with two diaper samples. Kevin could have thrown them away, thinking, "We don't need these." But when he saw those two diapers, something came alive on the inside. He took that as a sign from God. That was his headstone.

He ran in and told Lisa, "We just got the first diapers for our babies." Then he wrote the date on those diapers and placed them on his desk. Month after month, he saw those diapers over and over. When you see something long enough, it eventually gets into your subconscious mind and drops down into your spirit. Then you know it's going to happen.

Several years later, Kevin and Lisa received a phone call out of the blue asking if they would be interested in adopting a baby. They said, "Yes, we would." The lady said, "How about adopting two? These are twin girls who are about to be born." Today Kevin and Lisa have their twins. They are teenagers now and as beautiful as can be.

Do you have something in front of you that represents the final piece to your dreams?

TODAY'S PRAYER

Father in Heaven, thank You that I have the assurance that the work You have started to do in my life will be brought to completion by Your love and power. I believe I can and will become everything You created me to be. Amen.

———— ◆ ————

TODAY'S THOUGHT

Don't let what people say about you or what they say to you hold you back from achieving your dream. Let your vision be the promise from God of what you will one day be or do.

Keep Your Vision in Front of You

Scripture Reading: Hebrews 11

Where there is no vision, the people perish.
Proverbs 29:18 KJV

Is there something you see every day that reminds you of what you're believing for, something that inspires you, ignites your faith? Proverbs says that without a vision you'll get stuck. That's why many people have lost their passion. They don't have anything that reminds them of what they're dreaming about.

In 1959, my parents started Lakewood Church in an old rundown feed store. They had ninety people. You know what my father called the church? Lakewood International Outreach Center. He put a big blue sign outside that cost more than the building. He put a big world map on one of the walls and a globe behind him when he spoke. He always had the world on his mind. The truth is, they were a small neighborhood church. But every time my father saw the sign, his vision increased. He was moving toward it.

When the ninety members saw the sign week after week, something was being birthed on the inside. Seeds of increase were taking root. Do you know what Lakewood is today? It is an international outreach center touching the world. One year at a conference, people came from 150 countries. It looked like the United Nations.

What are you believing God for? Keep your vision in front of you.

A friend of mine who wanted a child decorated her baby's room, bought a bed and stroller, and spent all this time, money, and energy. Her friends thought she was a little far out, but she understood that what you keep in front of you, you are moving toward. A year went by, and still no baby. Two years, no baby. Five years. Ten years. She didn't get discouraged. When she'd walk by the baby's room, the seed was growing. She kept thanking God that her baby was on the way. It didn't look like anything was happening, but she was moving toward it. Twenty years later she had not one baby, but two babies!

If you're believing to move into a nicer house, find a picture of a house you like and put it on your bathroom mirror. Let that seed get into you. If you're believing to get into a college, go buy the school's T-shirt and wear it around. Every time you see that picture or that T-shirt, say under your breath: "Thank You, Lord, for bringing my dreams to pass. Thank You, Lord, that I'll become everything You created me to be."

What you keep in front of you, you're moving toward.

TODAY'S PRAYER

Father, help me to keep the vision in front of me and to know that You are bringing my dreams to pass. My hopes and dreams are in Your hands. I trust You. In Jesus' Name. Amen.

TODAY'S THOUGHT

Do not worry. Do not doubt. Keep your trust in God, knowing that He cannot fail you. He will give birth to every promise He puts in your heart.

Release Your Faith in a Big Way

Scripture Reading: Ephesians 3

*Now to Him who is able to do exceedingly
abundantly above all that we ask or think,
according to the power that works in us . . .*
Ephesians 3:20–21 NKJV

Don't have just a little vision of what God can do for you. You're not inconveniencing God to believe big. In fact, when you believe to do great things, it pleases God.

Take the limits off and say, "I don't see a way, but God, I know You have a way, so I'm going to believe to start a business to impact the world. I will believe that my whole family will serve You. I will believe to get totally well."

It doesn't matter what it looks like in the natural; God is a supernatural God. He's not limited by your resources, by your environment, by your education, or by your nationality. If you'll have a big vision, God will not only do what you're dreaming about, He will do more than you can ask or think.

A few years after my father went to be with the Lord and I stepped up to pastor the church, I had a desire to write a book. My dad had written many books, and they were all translated into Spanish. On the bookshelf I walk by at home every day, I had two copies of my dad's most popular book. One was in English. The other was in Spanish. I kept those books in front of me, knowing one day at the right time I would write a book. My dream was that it, too, would be translated into Spanish.

In my mind this seemed so far out. I never thought I could get up and minister, much less write a book. This was stretching my faith. A year went by, no book. Two years, three years, four years. It would have been easy to lose my passion and think it was never going to happen. But I had my father's books strategically placed on this bookshelf right outside my closet. I saw them thousands of times. I didn't always consciously think about them, but even subconsciously I was moving toward writing my own. My faith was being released. Something on the inside was saying, "Yes, one day I'm going to write a book."

In 2004, I wrote my first book, *Your Best Life Now*. When the publisher read the manuscript, they decided to publish it in English and Spanish at the same time. Normally they wait to see if anybody buys it in English. But that's the way God is. His dream for your life is bigger than your own.

TODAY'S PRAYER

Father, thank You that You give me not just exceedingly and abundantly, but exceedingly abundantly above all I can ask or think. Help me to keep growing in the revelation of Your love and to be bold to ask big and think big. I believe that You have amazing plans for my life. Amen.

TODAY'S THOUGHT

God is a supernatural God who will open up doors for you. He will surround you with His favor and speak to the right people about you. He has amazing blessings in your future.

God Will Supersize Your Vision

Scripture Reading: 2 Kings 4

. . . we're never left feeling shortchanged.
Quite the contrary—we can't round up enough
containers to hold everything God generously pours
into our lives through the Holy Spirit!
Romans 5:5 MSG

I've found that whatever your vision is, God will supersize it. He will do more than you can ask or think. My vision was that my first book would be so well received it would be translated into Spanish. But it was also translated into French, German, Russian, Swahili, Portuguese, and more than forty other languages.

If you keep the vision in front of you and not get talked out of it, but just keep honoring God, being your best, thanking Him that it's on the way, God will supersize whatever you're believing for. He'll do exceedingly abundantly above and beyond.

I saw an article in the paper several years ago about a man who gave a university one hundred million dollars. I cut that article out and put it on my desk. Every time I see it, I say, "God, You did it for a university. You can do it for a ministry."

I have a big vision. We can reach a lot of people with an extra one hundred million. If you can accomplish your dreams in your own strength, talent, ability, and resources, your dreams are too small. You don't need God's help with small dreams.

Believe big. Your destiny is too great, your assignment too important, to have little goals, little dreams, little prayers.

Keep big things in front of you. A friend of mine and his wife support orphanages and feed a million children every day. That's what I keep in front of me. In our kitchen at home, we have pictures of some of the children we sponsor through our partner World Vision. Every time we eat dinner, we say, "God, You did it for them. You can do it for us. Let our family impact millions of children." We're moving toward it.

You may say, "Well, Joel, I can't even imagine that happening to me." Don't worry—you won't be. If you don't have a vision for it, it's not going to happen. Without a vision you won't see God's best. You won't be the winner He wants you to be.

TODAY'S PRAYER

Father, thank You that You are El Shaddai, the God Who is more than enough. This is my year to see You supersize my vision. I am moving forward and making room for Your far-and-beyond favor. Help me to step into the abundance You have in store. Amen.

TODAY'S THOUGHT

Make sure you don't shortchange yourself. Don't limit your vision. You may not see how it could happen. That's okay; that's not your job. Your job is to believe. God has a thousand ways to fill your containers that you've never thought of.

Use the Power of Your Imagination

Scripture Reading: John 5

Jesus looked at them and said,
"With man this is impossible, but with
God all things are possible."
Matthew 19:26

Some things may seem very unlikely, but don't ever say, "I can't imagine that for me." You see somebody really fit when you're trying to get back in shape and you may think: "I can't imagine looking like that." You may drive by a nice house and say, "I can't imagine living in this neighborhood, owning my own business, or being that successful."

The problem is you're being limited by your own imagination. You've got to change what you're seeing. Don't let negative thoughts paint those pictures. Use your imagination to see yourself accomplishing dreams, rising higher, overcoming obstacles, and being healthy, strong, blessed, and prosperous.

I don't say this arrogantly, but I can imagine my books being published in every language. I can imagine somebody handing us that one-hundred-million-dollar check. I can imagine us feeding a million children a day. I can imagine living a long, healthy life.

Not only that, I can imagine you fulfilling your dreams. I can imagine you totally out of debt, healthy and strong, and leading your company. I can imagine you blessing the world, being a history maker, and setting a new standard for your family. Now I'm asking you not only to have it in your imagination, but to also keep something in front of you that reminds you of it.

Perhaps you need to lose thirty pounds. Why don't you put up a picture of yourself thirty pounds lighter on your bathroom mirror? Every day when you see it, say, "Lord, thank You that I'm losing this weight. I'm healthy, whole, strong, in shape, energetic, attractive." Let that new image take root.

You may not be healthy today, but you need to keep something in front of you that says you're going to be healthy. Put up pictures of yourself when you were healthy and strong all over your house. Put up Scripture verses. Check on that gym you want to join.

Keep the right vision in front of you. You can. You will!

TODAY'S PRAYER

Father, I would like to take the limits off of You and release my imagination to believe You for the extraordinary. I want to believe that You will increase me and show me Your favor. I believe that You are taking me forward into the fullness of my destiny. Amen.

TODAY'S THOUGHT

You may have struggled with your weight, your health, your finances, or with a relationship for a long time, and you keep wondering, "Will this ever change?" God is saying, "Keep the right vision in front of you. You can. You will!"

Release Your Faith

Scripture Reading: Deuteronomy 7

It was because the LORD loved you . . . that he brought you out with a mighty hand and redeemed you from the land of slavery . . . Know therefore that the LORD your God is God; he is the faithful God, keeping his covenant of love . . .

Deuteronomy 7:8–9

A man in our church started a company that specializes in drilling for oil with just himself and one assistant. It grew and grew. He was spending a lot of his time traveling around checking on the different sites. One day he saw a competitor's employees boarding their company airplane, doing what he did in a fraction of the time. God dropped the dream in his heart that he could have an airplane.

When his family members heard him talking about having an airplane, they thought he'd lost his mind. They couldn't imagine it, but he could. Sometimes your family will not encourage you. You've got to listen to what God's telling you and not to what other people may tell you. People will try to talk you out of your dreams.

My friend bought a model of the airplane he wanted and put it on his desk. When people asked, "What's that plane for?" he told them, "That's my airplane. That's what I'm going to use to travel the country." Year after year he kept that plane in front of him.

One day the competitor that he'd seen flying around walked into his office and said, "I'm retiring. I'd like to sell you my airplane." My friend couldn't afford that beautiful twelve-seat plane. He was hoping to buy a little, used two-seat plane. He said, "I appreciate the offer, but I don't have those kinds of funds." The competitor said, "Sure you do. Just take over my monthly payments, and you can have the plane."

My friend got that big, beautiful plane for a fraction of the value, and today he flies all over the world. He said, "Joel, God has done more than I ever imagined."

When you keep your vision in front of you, that's your faith being released. That's why the Scriptures use such strong language that says people perish for lack of vision. That means dreams die when you don't have vision. If you can't see what God has put in your heart, you'll miss the incredible things God wants to do.

TODAY'S PRAYER

Father in Heaven, I thank You that the fulfillment of my dreams is on the way, even the secret petitions of my heart. You spoke the worlds into existence, and You have me in the palm of Your hand. I believe You will make sure I complete what You put me here to do. Amen.

TODAY'S THOUGHT

The moment God put a dream in your heart, the moment the promise took root, God not only started it, but He set a completion date. God will bring your dreams to pass. Now do your part and break out of anything holding you back. Pray God-sized prayers.

Look at the Stars

Scripture Reading: Genesis 15

[The LORD] took him outside and said, "Look up at the sky and count the stars—if indeed you can count them." Then he said to him, "So shall your offspring be." Abram believed the LORD, and he credited it to him as righteousness.

Genesis 15:5–6

In the Scriptures, God promised Abraham that he would be the father of many nations. In the natural it was impossible. Abraham didn't have one child. He was eighty years old. But God didn't just give him the promise; God gave him a picture to look at.

God said, "Abraham, go out and look at the stars—that's how many descendants you will have." God told him also to look at the grains of sand at the seashore, because that was how many relatives he would have. Why did God give him pictures? God knew there would be times when it would look as if the promise would not come to pass, and Abraham would be discouraged and tempted to give up.

In those times, Abraham would go out at night and look up at the sky. When he saw the stars, faith would rise in his heart. Something would tell him, "It's going to happen. I can see it." And in the morning when his thoughts told him, "You're too old, it's too late, you heard God wrong," he would go down to the beach and look at the grains of sand. His faith would be restored.

Like Abraham, there will be times when it seems as if your dreams are not coming to pass. It's taking so long. The medical report doesn't look good. You don't have the resources. Business is slow. You could easily give up.

But like Abraham, you've got to go back to that picture. Keep that vision in front of you. When you see the key to your new house, the tennis shoes for when you're healthy, the picture frame for your spouse, or the article inspiring you to build an orphanage, those pictures of what you're dreaming about will keep you encouraged.

God is saying to you what He said to Abraham: "If you can see it, I can do it. If you have a vision for it, I can make a way. I can open up new doors. I can bring the right people. I can give you the finances. I can break the chains holding you back."

TODAY'S PRAYER

Father, You are the all-powerful sovereign Lord of the universe. My dreams are not too big and the challenges in my life are not too difficult. You have a way to bring them to pass. I believe that what You have promised You will do. Amen.

TODAY'S THOUGHT

Stop spending so much time analyzing your situation. You may have so many facts and figures that you've talked yourself out of what God can do. God asked Abraham, "Is anything too hard for the Lord?" That faith will keep you fully persuaded that God will make a way, even though you don't see a way.

Your Dreams Will Fall into Place

Scripture Reading: Luke 5

*When he had finished speaking, he said to Simon,
"Put out into deep water, and let down the nets for a catch."
Simon answered, "Master, we've worked hard all night and
haven't caught anything. But because you say so, I will let down
the nets." When they had done so, they caught such a large
number of fish that their nets began to break.*

Luke 5:4–6

As a young man back in the 1930s, Conrad Hilton saw an article about the Waldorf Astoria Hotel in New York City. The article said it was the most famous hotel in the world and included big, beautiful pictures. Hilton had never seen anything like that grand, magnificent hotel. As he was reading the article, God put the dream in his heart to one day own that hotel. In the natural, it didn't seem possible. He could barely pay his rent. He didn't have any connections. The Great Depression was just ending.

He could have said, "God, You have the wrong person." Instead, he dared to let the seed take root. He cut out the picture of the beautiful Waldorf and put it under the glass on his desk. Every day he would see that picture for one year, two years, five years, ten years. It did not look like his dream would happen, but he kept that vision in front of him.

When he went to New York City, he walked around the Waldorf Astoria Hotel and prayed. He thanked God that it was his—but he did not tell anyone; he just let the dream take root. Eighteen years later, his company was able to purchase nearly

250,000 shares of the Waldorf Corporation, and Hilton owned the most famous hotel in the world.

Friends, what you keep in front of you, you're moving toward. You may think it's too late—your dreams are too big, your obstacles too difficult—but God is still on the throne. He still has a way to bring them to pass. God will do something big in your life. What you thought was over and done is still going to happen. When it looks impossible, God will suddenly cause things to fall into place, giving you favor, influence, and connections.

Don't stop believing. Every time you see your vision, you're moving toward it. Thank God that it's on the way. If you'll do this, God will supersize what you're dreaming about. He will take you further faster, opening doors that no man can shut, doing what medicine cannot do. I believe and declare that every dream, every promise, every goal God put in your heart, He will bring to pass.

TODAY'S PRAYER

Father in Heaven, you are the Great I Am who provides everything I need. I don't know how my dreams can come to pass, but I trust You. My life is in Your hands. I believe that I have exactly what I need to fulfill my destiny. In Jesus' Name. Amen.

TODAY'S THOUGHT

Right now God is breathing on your dreams. He will multiply your talent, your resources, and your creativity. This is not the time to shrink back in fear. This is the time to move forward in faith.

SECTION 2

Run Your
RACE

Live to Please God, Not People

Scripture Reading: Romans 12

And do not be conformed to this world,
but be transformed by the renewing of your mind,
that you may prove what is that good and
acceptable and perfect will of God.

Romans 12:2 NKJV

There will always be people who try to squeeze you into their molds and pressure you into being who they want you to be. They may be good people who mean well, but the problem is they didn't breathe life into you, equip you, or empower you. God did.

If you're going to become the winner you were created to be, you need to be bold. The second quality of a winner is that you run your race the way you want to run it. You can't be insecure, and you can't worry about what everyone thinks. You can't try to keep everyone happy. If you change with every criticism and try to win their favor, you'll go through life letting people manipulate you and pressure you into their boxes.

You have to accept the fact that you can't keep everyone happy or win over every critic. Even if you changed and did everything they asked, some would still find fault. You're not really free until you're free from trying to please everyone. You're respectful and kind, but you're not living to please people; you're living to please God.

Every morning when you get up, you should search your heart. Know deep down that you're being true to who God called you to be. Then you won't have to look to the left or to the right. Just stay focused on your goals. If people get upset because you don't fit into their mold, that's okay. If you lose a friend because you won't let that person control you, that person was not a true friend. If people are jealous, critical, and try to make you look bad, don't let that change you. You don't need their approval when you have God's.

Instead of running our races, we often make decisions based on superficial things. We spend too much time trying to impress people, trying to gain their approval, wondering what they're going to think if we take this job or wear a new outfit or move into a new neighborhood. If you will get free from what everyone else thinks and start being who you were created to be, you will rise to a new level.

TODAY'S PRAYER

Father, thank You that You called me to be the person You want and made me to be. I want my life to be fully pleasing to You, and I ask You to transform me through the renewing of my mind so that I will know and be able to walk in Your will and ways. Amen.

TODAY'S THOUGHT

Don't be held back by the fear of others' disapproval when you don't fit their mold. If they leave you, God said He would never leave us nor forsake us. If someone withholds approval, it's no big deal because you have God's approval.

Be Who You Were Created to Be

*"Now when David had served God's purpose
in his own generation, he fell asleep . . ."*

Acts 13:36

I read an interesting report from a nurse who asked hundreds of patients facing death what their biggest regrets were. The number one regret was: "I wish I had been true to who I was and not just lived to meet the expectations of others."

How many people today are not being true to who they are because they're afraid they may disappoint someone or fall out of their good graces? I say this respectfully, but you can't live the life God wanted for you if you are trying to be who your parents or your friends want you to be. You have to be true to who God made you to be.

When my father went to be with the Lord, I realized that my life purpose was different from my father's. His calling was to help bring down church denominational walls, and he traveled the world telling people about the fullness of the Spirit.

When I took over our church, I felt pressured to be like my father, to minister and run the church like him. But when I searched my heart, deep down I knew my calling was to plant a seed of hope, to encourage people, to let them know about the goodness of God.

It was a struggle, because I loved my father. Some people had been at the church for forty years. I thought, "What will people think? They may not accept me." But one day I read a scripture about David. It said, "David fulfilled God's purpose for his generation."

I heard God say right down in my heart: "Joel, your dad fulfilled his purpose. Now quit trying to be like him, and go out and fulfill your purpose." When I heard that, it was as if a light turned on. I realized, "I don't have to be like my father. I don't have to fit into a certain mold. It's okay to run my race. I am free to be me."

After all, God doesn't want you to be an imitation of someone else. You should be the original you were created to be. There is an anointing on your life, an empowerment, not to be somebody else, but to be you. If you let people squeeze you into their molds and you bow down to their pressure to try to please your critics, it not only takes away your uniqueness, but it also lessens the favor on your life.

TODAY'S PRAYER

Father, today I seek first Your kingdom and what You want me to be. I release those who do not support what You've placed in my heart. I forgive them and love them. Thank You for rewarding me as I seek You alone. Amen.

———— ✦ ————

TODAY'S THOUGHT

If you are to become all God created you to be, you can't let a hurt, a loss, or someone else's disapproval of you cause you to sit on the sidelines. Be the original you were created to be. Keep standing, keep believing, because soon you will rise up into the higher places He has in store for you.

Run with Purpose

Scripture Reading: John 12

*". . . for they loved human praise more
than praise from God."*
John 12:43

After I took over our church, there were several members who had been with the church for a long time, friends of the family for years, who were upset because I wasn't exactly like my father. When I wouldn't let them squeeze me into their mold, they left our church, which was difficult for me. I wanted their approval. But looking back now, I believe one reason God has promoted me is because I tuned out all the negative voices and I've done my best to stay true to who God made me to be.

Jesus talked about those who loved the praise of people more than the praise of God. One of the tests we all have to pass is when someone in our lives whom we respect and look up to wants us to go one direction, when we know in our hearts that we should take another path. We want their approval, but if we are to fulfill our destinies, we have to be strong. We have to have this attitude: "I want the praise of God more than the praise of people. I have a purpose. I will become who God created me to be."

I've learned if you please God and stay true to what He's put in your heart, eventually you will have the praise of people. His favor, His anointing, and His blessing will cause you to excel. People may not understand why you don't take their advice, but later they'll see you walking in the fullness of your destiny. You will see new opportunities, new relationships. God's favor on your life will increase if you quit worrying about what everyone thinks and do what God has put in your heart.

People will tell you how to run your life. If you try to please everyone, I can guarantee you one thing 100 percent: You'll be confused, frustrated, and miserable.

I live by this motto: Everyone has a right to an opinion, and I have every right to not listen to it. If what others say doesn't match what God has put in your heart, let it go in one ear and out the other. I don't look to the left or to the right. I run my race. I don't try to compete with anyone else. I don't let people control me and go around feeling guilty because I don't fit into their boxes. I don't get upset if something negative is said about me. I look straight ahead and, as the apostle Paul said, I run with purpose in every step.

TODAY'S PRAYER

Father, thank You for leading and guiding me with Your peace and joy. Help me to stay true to pleasing You and You alone so that I can run my race, fulfill my destiny, and live the life You have in store for me. In Jesus' Name. Amen.

TODAY'S THOUGHT

There is real freedom when you realize that you don't need other people's approval because you have almighty God's approval. Run your own race and refuse to be controlled by what others' think and say.

Thanks, but No Thanks

Scripture Reading: Galatians 1

*Am I now trying to win the approval of human beings,
or of God? Or am I trying to please people?
If I were still trying to please people,
I would not be a servant of Christ.*

Galatians 1:10

I heard about this man who fell into a pit, and while he was down there, several people came by and offered their opinions.

The Pharisee said, "You deserve to be in the pit."

The Catholic said, "You need to suffer while you're in the pit."

The Baptist said, "If you had been saved, you wouldn't have fallen into the pit."

The charismatic said, "Just confess I'm not in the pit."

The mathematician said, "Let me calculate how you fell into the pit."

The IRS agent said, "Have you paid taxes on that pit?"

The optimist said, "Things could be worse."

The pessimist said, "Things will get worse."

Everyone has an opinion. If you try to keep every person happy, the one person who will not be happy is you. Sometimes those who try to run your life and tell you what to do can't even run their own lives, much less yours.

It's fine to listen to opinions. It's great to receive advice, but you have to be secure enough in who God made you to be so that when something doesn't bear witness with your spirit, you'll have a boldness that says, "Thanks, but no thanks. I appreciate your advice, I value your opinion, but that's not for me."

TODAY'S PRAYER

Father, thank You for approving and loving me. Because I have Your approval, I don't have to live for the approval of others. Help me to walk in the security of Your love as I step forward into the destiny You have prepared for me. Amen.

TODAY'S THOUGHT

Don't be held in check by the negative voices and naysayers who would put you and keep you in a box of their own design. Your destiny is too great for that. Keep being your best, and nothing can stop you.

Beware of Controllers

Scripture Reading: Hebrew 12

And let us run with perseverance the race marked out for us,
fixing our eyes on Jesus, the pioneer and perfecter of faith. . . .
Consider him who endured such opposition from sinners,
so that you will not grow weary and lose heart.

Hebrews 12:1–3

While you have to be aware of the influence of others over you, that is especially true of high-maintenance people. These people are almost impossible to keep happy. You've got to call them on their schedule, keep them cheered up, run their errands, and meet their demands. If not, they're upset and disappointed. And they'll do their best to make sure you feel guilty.

High-maintenance people are almost always controllers. If you're not careful, they'll squeeze you into their mold. They're not interested in you. They're interested in what you can do for them.

If you fall into the trap of always trying to please a controller, you will wear yourself out and constantly be frustrated. Years ago, I went out of my way to help this couple who were friends. They moved to another city, and I gave them money to help them move. I called and checked on them. If they needed anything, I was always available.

Even so, I got the feeling from them that I was never doing enough. They were never satisfied. They always had a complaint. I had gone out of my way to be kind and generous, but they were constantly finding fault and trying to make me feel guilty.

One day I realized they were just high-maintenance people and I was not responsible for making them happy. I couldn't make them decide to like me. I had to run my race and not let them steal my joy. That was a great day in my life!

Your time is too valuable to worry about pleasing everyone else or making them happy. I know people who spend more time worrying about what others think about them than they do focusing on their own dreams and goals. You have to get free from that.

TODAY'S PRAYER

Father, help me to choose my relationships wisely.
Empower me with boldness to walk away from those
who are dragging me down and stealing my joy.
I want to run the race that You've set before me.
Help me to fix my eyes upon You. Amen.

TODAY'S THOUGHT

Some people never reach their highest potential
because they never get away from the controllers
who abuse their kindness. Don't enable another person's
dysfunction. Be kind, but show them the door.

It's Not about You

Scripture Reading: Acts 5:12–42

Peter and the other apostles replied:
"We must obey God rather than human beings! . . .
We are witnesses of these things, and so is the Holy Spirit,
whom God has given to those who obey him."
Acts 5:29, 32

If you're going to do anything great in life, not everyone will cheer you on. Your family, friends, and coworkers may not celebrate you. Some won't be able to handle your success as God pours out His favor. Some may be jealous and try to discredit you, belittle you, or won't give you the time of day, or maybe a friend you've been good to for years won't understand you. Let that bounce off you like water off a duck's back. If you don't, you'll start changing, being defensive, thinking that you've got to prove to them that you're really okay. What you're doing is letting them squeeze you into their mold.

Your destiny is too great to get distracted trying to win over people. Don't take it personally. It's not about you. It's about the favor God put on your life. It stirs up the jealousy in them. Until they deal with it, nothing you can do will change it. Shake it off and run your race, because no matter what you do, they will still find fault. No matter how much you try to show them kindness, they will still find some reason to be critical.

It's like a country grandfather I heard about who took his grandson to town on a donkey. He started off letting his grandson ride the donkey as he walked alongside. Somebody passed by and said, "Look at that selfish boy making that old man walk." The grandfather heard it and took the boy off. Then he rode the donkey as his grandson walked by his side, but somebody said, "Look at that man making that little boy walk while he rides." Hearing that, the grandfather pulled the little boy up with him, and they both rode the donkey. Then another person said, "How cruel of them to place such a heavy load on the donkey." By the time they got to town, the grandfather and grandson were carrying the donkey!

The point is that no matter what you do, you will never please everybody. Even when you do your best, some will find fault with you, and that's okay. They have a right to have their opinions, and you have a right to ignore them.

TODAY'S PRAYER

Father, thank You for the gifts and callings You have placed on my life. I choose to be faithful to You, as the apostles were in Acts 5, even when other people don't approve. Thank You for the favor that You are pouring out upon my life and the successes You are giving me. Amen.

TODAY'S THOUGHT

When God sends people into your life, you don't need to walk on eggshells trying not to offend them. You don't have to bend to their beliefs. If someone tries to squeeze you into their mold, let go and walk away.

Take Control of Your Happiness

Scripture Reading: Proverbs 19

A hot-tempered person must pay the penalty;
rescue them, and you will have to do it again.
Proverbs 19:19

Too many people sacrifice their own happiness to keep some-one else happy. They've got to stop by their friend's house and say hello, because they don't want to upset the friend. They stay late at night in the office to keep the boss happy. They've got to loan their friend money, because the friend is in trouble again. If they don't meet all the demands and fix this person, rescue this person, solve this person's problem, then they'll fall out of somebody's good grace, and that somebody won't understand and will get upset.

But God did not call you to keep everyone happy. It's good to be loving, kind, and generous, but you are not responsible for the happiness of others. You are responsible for your own happiness.

You may feel that if you don't meet all their demands and needs, if you don't rescue them or loan them money, then they'll be angry with you. But if that's the case, maybe it's time for them to be unhappy instead of you. If they get mad, they're manipulators. They are using you.

Your time is too valuable to go through life letting people control you and make you feel guilty if you don't come running every time they call. The easy thing is to just give in and keep bailing them out, so you don't make any waves.

But as long as you rescue them and you're there to cheer them up and keep them all fixed up, you're not really helping them. You're a crutch. Because of you, they don't have to deal with the real issues. You're enabling their dysfunction.

The only way these dependent people will get the help they need is for you to stop being their crutch. Don't come running every time they have an "emergency."

Put your foot down and say, "I love you, but I'm not going to let you control me. I love you, but I'm not jumping every time you call. I love you, but I refuse to feel guilty if I don't meet all your demands."

TODAY'S PRAYER

Father, today I submit to You every relationship in my life.
I trust that You will give me wisdom to see clearly
where I am enabling others in their dysfunction and
give me boldness to stop being their crutch. Amen.

———— ◆ ————

TODAY'S THOUGHT

You want people in your life who are supposed to be there,
not those who expect you to meet their demands and needs.
You are not responsible for the happiness of others.
Put your foot down and refuse to be a crutch.

You Are Not the Savior

Scripture Reading: Judges 16

The fear of human opinion disables;
trusting in God protects you from that.
Proverbs 29:25 MSG

If people are controlling you, it's not their fault; it's your fault. You have to set some boundaries. Quit allowing them to call you all hours of the day to dump their problems on you. That's why we have voice mail!

Quit caving in to them every time they throw a fit. Ignore it. Quit loaning them money every time they make poor choices. Don't take on a false sense of responsibility. You are not the savior of the world. We already have a Savior. You're not supposed to keep everyone happy or fixed. If you take on that job, the one person who will not be happy is you.

Years ago I knew this man who was always having problems paying his rent. My heart went out to him, and I helped him again and again. Every other month he would claim that something had come up that kept him from making his payment. After about the fifth emergency request for rent money, I started to wise up.

He told me a client hadn't paid him. He told me the check was in the mail but hadn't arrived. He also claimed a relative had become sick, and he'd been called out of town. His excuses went on and on.

At the end of another long, sad story, he said, "Now what are we going to do?"

I thought to myself, "We're not going to do anything because this is not my problem. This is your problem, and I'm not going to feel guilty because you keep making poor choices."

I believe I'd still be helping him today five years later if I had not put my foot down. When you refuse to keep helping people like that, you force them to look inside and take responsibility. A lot of times we do things out of guilt, because we think we'll feel bad if we don't help overly dependent or manipulative people.

But if they're not taking responsibility for their own lives, you're not helping them—you're hurting them. They need to deal with their own issues like most people. When you back away, it will force them to change.

TODAY'S PRAYER

Father, thank You that You have called me to help others fulfill Your plans for their lives, but not to make them happy or to fix them. You alone are our Savior. Help me to be loving and kind, but not manipulated by anyone. Amen.

TODAY'S THOUGHT

Sometimes you have to put up with others' difficulties and love them back to wholeness, but you can't spend your whole life knee-deep in their troubles. You can't fulfill your destiny if you are carrying them on your back. Be polite, but pull away.

Cut the Puppet Strings

Scripture Reading: Galatians 2

*This matter arose because some false believers
had infiltrated our ranks to spy on the freedom we have
in Christ Jesus and to make us slaves. We did not give in
to them for a moment, so that the truth of the gospel
might be preserved for you.*

Galatians 2:4–5

I've learned to recognize that some people are always having a crisis and in desperate need of something. It's good to help people who are in real need. But if someone comes to you a dozen times, and it seems the emergencies never stop, you need to recognize that's a manipulator and you are their puppet. They know if they pull one string, you'll feel guilty, or another string and you'll bail them out.

If someone is playing you like a puppet, it's time to cut the strings. No more letting them make you feel guilty. No more will you come running. You may feel you'll lose their friendship if you refuse to help them, but that feeling is your wakeup call. God just met your need. He just closed that door for you. The truth is if someone becomes upset because you won't meet unreasonable demands, that person is not your friend. That person is a manipulator. The sooner you break free, the better off you'll be.

Are you doing too much for other people and not enough for yourself? Are you so good-hearted that you're sacrificing your happiness to keep everyone around you happy? If you are giving all the time and not receiving back, you need to examine your relationships. They are out of balance. You shouldn't have to constantly meet the demands and needs of your friends out of fear of being rejected by them. If they give you the cold shoulder to make you feel guilty, they're not really friends.

If you allow it, people will try to run your life. Don't waste your life playing up to people, trying to meet all their demands, when the truth is they're not interested in you; they're interested in what you can do for them. Cut the puppet strings. You don't have time to play games, get entangled, or become distracted trying to keep everybody happy. You have a destiny to fulfill. Be bold, take charge of your life, and pursue the dreams God has placed in your heart.

TODAY'S PRAYER

Father, thank You that You did not make me to
be other people's puppet and try to please them by
fulfilling their wishes and demands. I want to be loving
and kind and help others who are in real need, but help me
to cut the strings of those who would manipulate and
use me to their own advantage. Amen.

TODAY'S THOUGHT

It's good to get free from addictions, free from anxiety,
and free from depression, but one of the greatest
freedoms is to get free from controlling people.

Quit Living on Eggshells

Scripture Reading: Titus 3

*I want you to put your foot down. Take a firm
stand on these matters so that those who have put their trust
in God will concentrate on the essentials that are good for
everyone. Stay away from mindless, pointless quarreling . . .
That gets you nowhere. Warn a quarrelsome person
once or twice, but then be done with him.*

Titus 3:8–10 MSG

When I was growing up, my grandfather would buy a new car every two years, and he would give his old car to one of us grandchildren. He was very generous. My junior year he gave me his Buick LeSabre. A friend of mine on the basketball team had a car as well. We decided to carpool. He lived fifteen minutes in the opposite direction of the school. I'd have to go get him and come all the way back. I didn't mind.

I drove one week, then he drove the next. We did this for a month or so with no problems, but then his car broke down one week, so I had to drive again. I had to take another of his weeks because his brother needed the car. It got to where I was driving all the time. I really didn't mind, but he wasn't very grateful; he acted like I owed it to him.

One day I asked him if he was planning on ever driving again. He told me how he was trying to keep the mileage down on his car and basically that I needed to keep picking him up, as though he was doing me a favor to let him ride in my car.

I did what I'm asking you to do. I told him very politely

that I wasn't able to come get him anymore. You would have thought I'd told him his life was ending. He gave me the biggest guilt trip and tried to make me feel as though I was such a selfish person. I thought, "That's fine with me. If you're only my friend if I meet your demands and cater to your every need, then good riddance. I don't need friends like that." I don't mind being good to people, but I do mind being used.

Quit letting others pressure you into being something that you're not. Quit living on eggshells because you don't want to fall out of their favor. Quit feeling afraid that if you don't perform perfectly, they'll be upset. Here's my message: Let them be upset. If you spend your life trying to please everyone and letting them control you, they may be happy but you'll end up missing your destiny. I'd rather please God and have some people upset with me than please people and have God upset with me.

TODAY'S PRAYER

Father, thank You that I never have to compromise myself in order to gain others' approval. It is only in You that I find my value and worth and joy. I believe that You have given me a destiny to fulfill and that I will discover true happiness as I pursue running my own life race. Amen.

TODAY'S THOUGHT

Don't try to talk or convince people into loving you. Don't let them make you into their crutch or allow them to be your crutch. Let them go. You don't need anyone else to fulfill your destiny.

Fly with Lifters and Thrusters

Scripture Reading: Acts 15

Barnabas wanted to take John along, the John nicknamed Mark. But Paul wouldn't have him; he wasn't about to take along a quitter who, as soon as the going got tough, had jumped ship on them in Pamphylia.

Acts 15:37–38 MSG

A pilot friend of mine told me there are four main principles to master when flying airplanes: lift, thrust, weight, and drag. You have to take all these into account to make sure the plane will fly.

These same principles apply to specific types of people. There are the lifters who brighten your day, cheer you up, and make you feel better about yourself. Then there are the thrusters who inspire you, motivate you, challenge you to move forward and pursue your dreams. The people in the third group are weights. They pull you down, dump their problems on you, so that you leave feeling heavier, negative, and discouraged. Finally, there are those who are a drag. They've always got a sad song. They're stuck in a pit. They expect you to cheer them up, fix their problems, and carry their loads.

We all encounter people from each of these four groups. You have to make sure you're spending the majority of your time with lifters and thrusters. If you're only hanging out with weights and drags, it will keep you from becoming everything you were created to be.

Some people have perpetual problems. If you allow them, they'll use you as a trash can to dump all their garbage in. You spend an hour with them and you feel like you've run a marathon. They're energy suckers. You leave them feeling drained and worn out.

You cannot continue to deal with them day after day if you expect to reach your highest potential. You won't lift off. You won't thrust forward into the good things God has in store if you're weighted down, letting people dump their loads on you.

You are not responsible for their happiness. Sure, there are times when we need to sow a seed and have a listening ear and take time to love people back into wholeness. But that should be for a season and not an ongoing drama. You can't allow someone to put negativity in you day after day if you expect to soar.

TODAY'S PRAYER

Father, thank You for the people You've brought
into my life who inspire and motivate me to become the
person You want me to be. Help me as I consider the people
with whom I am giving my time and energies. Show me
where I need to put up boundaries. Amen.

TODAY'S THOUGHT

God has placed people in your life to inspire you,
to challenge you, to help you grow and accomplish your
dreams. You don't need those who weigh you down and
dump their loads on you.

Carefully Evaluate the Negative

Scripture Reading: Mark 5

[Jesus] did not let anyone follow him except Peter,
James and John the brother of James.

Mark 5:37

You need to evaluate the people you're spending time with. Are they lifters and encouragers? Do they make you feel better? Do you leave their company feeling inspired and happier, or are they dragging you down, making you feel drained, and sapping your energy?

When I was in my early twenties, this young lady cut my hair. She was as nice as could be. She had a good heart, but she was so negative. Every time I went she told me all of her problems. This went on month after month and year after year. She claimed the shop owners weren't treating her right and made her work extra hours. She also complained about a sister who was causing her problems. She'd say she didn't know if she could pay her rent, and her father wasn't doing well.

Every time I left her shop I felt depressed. She was very convincing. I did my best to encourage her. I prayed with her. I gave her money. I sent her customers. But it was never enough.

One day I realized what I'm telling you: "I cannot get to where I'm going with her in my life. I love her. I will pray for her. But I cannot fulfill my destiny with that weight or that drag on me month after month."

I made a change. It was difficult. I don't like to hurt feelings, but I realized my assignment is too important and my time is too valuable to let people continually pull me down.

You may have to make changes where you do business, where you play ball, or where you work out. You may have to change the phone calls you take. You shouldn't spend an hour on the phone every night listening to somebody's woes or hearing their sad songs. Put an end to it. Be kind, be respectful, but you don't need that weight going into you.

TODAY'S PRAYER

Father in Heaven, I want to be loving and kind
and helpful, but I refuse to carry others' weights and
negativities. I am believing that You will open the door for
more lifters and thrusters in my life to keep me running
straight ahead. In Jesus' Name. Amen.

TODAY'S THOUGHT

If your friends and those in your inner circle are
not making you stronger and challenging you to grow
and fulfill your destiny, move them out. You can still be
friends from a distance, but spend your time with
those who really believe in you.

Be Strong in the Lord

Scripture Reading: 1 Chronicles 22

*Now set your mind and heart to seek (inquire of
and require as your vital necessity) the Lord your God.*
1 Chronicles 22:19 AMP

You need to be around lifters, thrusters, people who inspire you and motivate you. That's why so many are drawn to our ministry. There are enough weights, enough drags. I'm going to push you forward. If you get around me, I'm going to lift you, encourage you, and inspire you. I'm going to do my best to leave you better than you were before.

You may work around people who are a drag. You don't have a choice. Or you may go to school with people who are a weight. They're negative and sour. Here's the key: Before you leave home, get prayed up, praised up, and encouraged.

Set your mind that it's going to be a great day. You can't go into that negative environment in neutral. You've got to go in already filled up, already encouraged. Don't go with your guard down, stressed out from the traffic, worried about the deadline, or listening to depressing news reports.

If you're not on the offensive, the weights and the drags will pull you down. Maybe you've got a twenty-minute drive on the way to work or school. Put on some good praise music. Get your spirit man built up. Build up a grateful attitude. Thank God for what He's done. Put on a good teaching DVD, something that inspires and motivates you. Talk to yourself the right way: "This is going to be a great day. I'm strong in the Lord. I've got the favor of God. I can do all things through Christ. Something good is going to happen to me."

That's how you'll stay strong and not let the weights and drags pull you down. You've got to build up a resistance.

TODAY'S PRAYER

Father, today I choose to tune into Your Word and to hear Your voice and to worship You first. Help me to clearly re-ceive Your truth and be built up in my spirit man so that I can defeat the discouraging, negative thoughts that will come my way. In Jesus' Name. Amen.

TODAY'S THOUGHT

Never tune into the negative. Set your mind and heart to faith-filled thoughts and to dismiss the thoughts that are not productive and positive. Don't give them the time of day.

It's Time to Break Free

Though the fig tree does not bud and there are
no grapes on the vines, though the olive crop fails and
the fields produce no food, . . . yet I will rejoice in the LORD,
I will be joyful in God my Savior. The Sovereign LORD
is my strength; he makes my feet like the feet
of a deer, he enables me to tread on the heights.

Habakkuk 3:17–19

What happens if you live with someone who's a weight? Perhaps you're married to a weight or a drag. Now I'm getting real! You've got to do the same thing that I talked about in yesterday's reading: Take extra doses of praise, encouragement, and inspiration. Stay filled up.

While they're changing, don't let them steal your joy. Some people don't want to be happy. They're always in the pits. Living with them is like living in the pits. You've got to have the attitude: "If you don't want to be happy, that's fine, but you're not going to keep me from being happy. If you want to stay in the pits, that's your choice, but I'm not getting in the pits with you."

Take responsibility for your own happiness. Don't let their issues sour your life. Pray for them, be respectful, but don't become codependent. Don't let their problems become your problems. Don't let them keep you from your destiny. It's time to break free.

Is there something keeping you from being happy? Are you allowing somebody to control you or make you feel guilty if you don't meet all their demands? Cut the puppet strings. Set some boundaries. Don't miss your destiny trying to please everyone.

God did not call you to be unhappy. He does not want you to waste your life trying to keep someone else happy. Be kind. Be compassionate, but run your own race. Remember, you don't need people's approval; you have God's approval.

Be secure enough in who you are that you don't live to please people. As long as you're doing what God has put in your heart, you don't need to look to the left or the right. Stay focused on your goals, and God will get you to where you're supposed to be.

TODAY'S PRAYER

Father, today I make it my top priority to renew my thoughts in Your Word, to dwell on Your Word, which is the truth that sets me free. I choose to not let anyone sour my life and steal my joy. Thank You for Your love and setting me free! Amen.

TODAY'S THOUGHT

Fill your thoughts with the promises of God and what God says about you. He says, "You are forgiven. Your best days are in front of you. I will restore the years that the enemy has stolen." Live the abundant life He has for you.

EXPECT
GOOD
THINGS

Have an Attitude of Expectancy

Scripture Reading: Psalm 5

Surely, LORD, you bless the righteous;
you surround them with your favor as with a shield.
Psalm 5:12

Our expectations set the limits for our lives. If you expect little, you're going to receive little. If you don't anticipate things to get better, they won't. But if you expect more favor, more good breaks, a promotion, and an increase, you will see new levels of favor and success.

Every morning when you wake up, you should declare, "Something good is going to happen to me today." You have to set the tone at the beginning of each day. Then all through the day you should have this attitude of expectancy.

Like a little child waiting to open a gift, you should be on the lookout, thinking, "I can't wait to see what's going to happen"—not passive, but actively expecting.

Too many people drag around, thinking, "Nothing good ever happens to me." Instead, start looking for good breaks. Expect to be at the right place at the right time. Expect your dreams to come to pass. Expect to be a winner.

Don't walk into a room anticipating people to not like you. Don't go to the store believing that you won't find what you need. Don't interview for a job assuming not to get it. Your expectation is your faith at work. When you expect good breaks, expect people to like you, or expect to have a great year, you're releasing your faith. That's what allows good things to happen.

But your expectations work in both directions. If you get up in the morning and expect it to be a lousy day and expect no breaks and expect people to be unfriendly, you'll draw that in. Your faith is working. The problem is you're using it in the wrong direction.

You may have had disappointments and unfair situations, but don't make the mistake of living in a negative frame of mind. Instead of expecting more of the same, start expecting it to turn around. Don't think you will barely get by; know that you will excel. Don't expect to be overcome. Expect to be the overcomer.

TODAY'S PRAYER

Father, I'm upgrading my expectations today
and shaking off doubt, negativity, disappointments, self-pity,
little dreams, and little goals. You are El Shaddai, the
God Who is more than enough. This is my time to rise
to new levels of favor and success. Amen.

TODAY'S THOUGHT

Rise up each morning expecting to experience
the surpassing greatness of God's favor throughout the day.
He is directing your steps. In His perfect timing,
everything will turn out right.

Upgrade Your Expectations

Scripture Reading: Psalm 81

I am the Lord your God, who brought you up out of Egypt.
Open wide your mouth and I will fill it.
Psalm 81:10

A young person told me he was concerned about taking his final exams. He had studied, but every time he took an important test, he stressed out, couldn't remember what he had studied, and did poorly. "Will you pray for me? I know it's going to happen again."

He was already expecting to fail. I shared with him this principle and told him, "You've got to change your expectations. All through the day say to yourself: 'I'm going to remember everything that I've studied and do great on this test.'" He came back a few weeks later and said that was the best he had ever done on one of his exams.

Let me ask you, what are you expecting? Big things, little things, or nothing at all? It's easy to anticipate the worst. But if you'll switch over into faith and expect the best—to excel, to accomplish your dreams—you'll draw in blessings and favor.

Some people have had a negative mind-set so long they don't realize they're doing it. It's just natural to them. They assume the worst, and they usually get it.

I know a lady who has been through a lot of negative things in her life, and it was like she was on autopilot. She expected people to hurt her, and they usually did. She expected to get laid off from her job, and eventually she did. Her expectations were drawing in the negative. One day she learned this principle and started anticipating different things. She waited for the best instead of the worst. She expected to get good breaks. She expected people to like her. Today it's totally turned around. She's living a victorious life.

You may not always feel like it, but when you get up each day you need to remind yourself that you are more than a conqueror. Your greatest victories are still out in front of you. The right people, the right opportunities, the right breaks are already in your future.

Now go out and be excited about the day, expecting things to change in your favor. Your attitude should be: "I'm expecting good breaks, to meet the right people, to see an increase in business, to get my child back on track, and for my health to improve. I'm expecting to be at the right place at the right time."

TODAY'S PRAYER

Father, I believe that You want to do something new, something amazing in my life. You are the God of the breakthrough who has first place in my life. I believe that You are about to take me beyond the barriers of the past and help me to step into the abundance You have in store. Amen.

TODAY'S THOUGHT

Raise your level of expectancy. Quit limiting God with small-minded thinking and start believing Him for bigger and better things. He will take you places you've never dreamed of.

Expect Goodness and Mercy

Scripture Reading: Psalm 23

Surely your goodness and mercy shall follow me all the days of my life; and I will dwell in the house of the LORD forever.

Psalm 23:6 NKJV

A young man told me: "Joel, I don't want to expect too much. That way if it doesn't happen, I won't go to bed all disappointed."

That's no way to live. If you're not expecting increase, promotion, or good breaks, you're not releasing your faith. Faith is what causes God to act. If you expect a break and it doesn't happen, don't go to bed disappointed. Go to bed knowing you're one day closer to seeing it come to pass. Get up the next morning and do it again.

Winners develop this third undeniable quality of expecting good things. You can't be in neutral and hope to reach your full potential or have God's best. It's not enough to not expect anything bad; you have to aggressively expect good things. Are you expecting your dreams to come to pass? Do you expect this year will be better than last year? Are you expecting to live a healthy, blessed life? Pay attention to what you're expecting.

Maybe you have a desire to get married. Don't go around thinking: "I'll never meet anyone. It's been so long, and I'm getting too old." Instead, expect to be at the right place at the right time. Believe that divine connections will come across your path. Believe that the right person will be attracted to you.

"What if I do that and nothing happens?"

What if you do it and something does happen? I can tell you nothing will happen if you don't believe.

David said in the Psalms: "Surely goodness and mercy shall follow me all the days of my life." In the past you may have had disappointments and setbacks following you around, but you need to let go of what didn't work out. Let go of every mistake, and let go of every failure.

Expect goodness and mercy to follow you wherever you go. It's good to look back sometimes and just say, "Hey, goodness. Hey, mercy. How are you doing back there?"

TODAY'S PRAYER

Father, thank You that You control the whole universe
and nothing is too hard for You. I expect to see Your hand
of unprecedented favor working in ways exceedingly,
abundantly, above and beyond my greatest dreams.
In Jesus' Name. Amen.

TODAY'S THOUGHT

Instead of expecting to get the short end of the stick in life,
start expecting God's blessings to chase after you.
Instead of expecting to barely get by in life, start
expecting the goodness of God to overtake you.

Superabundance

Scripture Reading: Ephesian 3

*Now to Him Who, by (in consequence of) the
[action of His] power that is at work within us, is able to
[carry out His purpose and] do superabundantly, far over and
above all that we [dare] ask or think [infinitely beyond our
highest prayers, desires, thoughts, hopes, or dreams] . . .*

Ephesians 3:20 AMP

Some people don't realize that they're always looking for the next disaster, looking for the next failure, or looking for the next bad break. Change what you're looking for. Start looking for goodness, mercy, favor, increase, and promotion. That's what should be following you around.

One definition of hope is "the happy anticipation of something good." If you're anticipating something good, it's going to bring you joy. It will give you enthusiasm. When you're expecting your dreams to come to pass, you'll go out each day with a spring in your step. But if you're not anticipating anything good, you'll drag through life with no passion.

I don't say this arrogantly, but I expect people to like me. Maybe I'm naïve, but if I am, do me a favor and leave me in my ignorance. When I go somewhere, I don't have all these walls up. I'm not defensive, insecure, intimidated, or thinking, "They're not going to like me. They're probably talking about me right now."

I expect people to be friendly. I believe that when people turn on my television program they can't turn me off. I think when people see my book in the stores they'll be drawn to it.

I'm talking about having an attitude of expecting good things. You need to get your *expecter* out. Maybe you haven't used it for six years. You need to start expecting greater things.

There are new mountains to climb and new horizons to explore. Expect to rise higher. Expect to overcome every obstacle. Expect doors to open. Expect favor at work, favor at home, favor at the grocery store, and favor in your relationships.

TODAY'S PRAYER

Father, thank You that You have given me gifts
and talents that I have not tapped into and there are new
levels of my destiny to which You are taking me.
Thank You that You are opening new doors of opportunity,
helping me to overcome every obstacle, and taking me
where I could not have gone on my own. Amen.

TODAY'S THOUGHT

Get ready for the surpassing greatness of God's favor! He will do exceedingly, abundantly above all that you ask or think. His high favor abides on those who walk in faith.

Remember the Good

Scripture Reading: Psalm 16

You have made known to me the path of life;
you will fill me with joy in your presence, with
eternal pleasures at your right hand.

Psalm 16:11

When you've been through hurts, disappointments, and failures, you have to guard your mind. Be careful what you allow to play in your thoughts all day. Your memory is very powerful.

You can be driving in your car and remember a tender moment with your child. It may have happened five years ago: a hug, a kiss, or something funny they did. But when you remember the moment, a smile comes to your face. You'll feel the same emotions, the same warmth and joy, just as if it were happening again.

On the other hand, you could be enjoying the day; everything is fine, but then you start remembering some sad event when you weren't treated right or something unfair happened. Before long you'll be sad, discouraged, and without passion.

What made you sad? Dwelling on the wrong memories. What made you happy? Dwelling on the right memories. Research has found that your mind will naturally gravitate toward the negative. One study discovered that positive and negative memories are handled by different parts of the brain. A negative memory takes up more space because there's more to process. As a result, you remember negative events more than positive events.

The study said that a person will remember losing fifty dollars more than he'll remember gaining fifty dollars. The negative effect has a greater impact, carrying more weight than the positive.

I've experienced this myself. I can walk off the platform after speaking and a hundred people might tell me, "Joel, that was great today. I really got something out of it." But I'll be more likely to remember just one person who says, "I didn't understand it. That didn't do anything for me."

In the old days, the negative comment would be all I'd think about. I'd play it over and over in my mind. That's human nature. That's how negative memories are stored in our brain. The bad takes up more space than the good.

TODAY'S PRAYER

Father, thank You that Your mercies are new every morning and that I can discard the discouragement, guilt, and condemnation of the past. It's a new day, and I will keep my mind focused on the good things You have done in my life. Amen.

———— ◊ ————

TODAY'S THOUGHT

God is bigger than your past, your disappointments, and your problems. Refuse to be a captive to negative memories. Start focusing on your possibilities. Let hope fill your heart.

Tune into Good Memories

Scripture Reading: Psalm 48

Within your temple, O God,
we meditate on your unfailing love.
Psalm 48:9

When it comes to your memories, you have to be proactive. When negative memories come back to the movie screen of the mind, many people pull up a chair, get some popcorn, and watch it all again as they lament the wrongs done to them.

Instead, remember this: That's not the only movie playing. There's another channel that is not playing back your defeats, your failures, or your disappointments. This channel features your victories, your accomplishments, and the things you did right. The good-memory channel plays back the times you were promoted, you met the right person, you bought a great house, and your children were healthy and happy.

Instead of staying on the negative channel, switch over to your victory channel. You will not move forward into better days if you're always replaying the negative things that have happened. We've all been through loss, disappointments, and bad breaks. So those memories will come to mind most often. The good news is you have the remote control. Change the channel. Don't dwell on negatives.

A couple of years after my father died, I stopped by my mother's house to pick up something. Nobody was home. As I walked through the den, I immediately recalled the night my father died of a heart attack in that very room. I could see him lying on the floor. The paramedics were shocking him, trying to get his heart to restart. That whole night played out in my mind, and I could feel the same emotions.

Then I did what I'm asking you to do. I said, "No thanks, I'm not going there. I'm not reliving that night. I'm not feeling those same sad and depressing emotions." I chose to change the channel. I started remembering all the great times we had together: the times we traveled the world together, and the times my father played with our son, Jonathan.

There was another channel. I just had to switch to it. Do you need to start changing the channel? Are you reliving every hurt, disappointment, and bad break? As long as you're replaying the negative, you will never fully heal. It's like a scab that's starting to get better, but it will only get worse if you pick at it.

TODAY'S PRAYER

Father, thank You that because I am Your child,
I can break free from what has been in the past and be healed.
I'm pressing forward and taking new ground, believing for
bigger things. Because Your face is shining on me
right now, who dares be against me?

TODAY'S THOUGHT

Switching channels is a decision you have to make. Today can
be a turning point in your life. Drop any emotional baggage
you're dragging and step toward a rich, full life! Trust God
and step into the great future He has for you.

A Garment of Praise

Scripture Reading: Isaiah 61

*He has sent me to bind up the brokenhearted,
to proclaim freedom for the captives and release from
darkness for the prisoners, to proclaim the year of the Lord's
favor . . . , to bestow on them a crown of beauty instead of ashes,
the oil of joy instead of mourning, and a garment
of praise instead of a spirit of despair.*

Isaiah 61:1–3

Emotional wounds are a powerful force in our lives and hold the potential to severely stifle our growth. If you're always reliving your hurts and watching them on the movie screen of your mind—talking about them and telling your friends—that's just reopening the wound. You have to change the channel. When you look back over your life, can you remember one time where you know it was the hand of God, promoting and protecting you? Switch over to that channel. Get your mind going in a new direction.

A reporter asked me not long ago what my biggest failure or regret has been. I don't mean to sound arrogant, but I don't remember what my biggest failure was. I don't dwell on that. I'm not watching that channel.

We all make mistakes. We all do things we wish we had done differently. You can learn from your mistakes, but you're not supposed to keep them in the forefront of your mind. You're supposed to remember the things you did right: The times you succeeded. The times you overcame the temptation. The times you were kind to strangers.

Some people are not happy because they remember every mistake they've made since 1927. They've got a running list. Do yourself a big favor and change the channel. Quit dwelling on how you don't measure up and how you should have been more disciplined, should have stayed in school, or should have spent more time with your children.

You may have fallen down, but focus on the fact that you got back up. You're here today. You may have made a poor choice, but dwell on your good choices. You may have some weaknesses, but remember your strengths. Quit focusing on what's wrong with you and start focusing on what's right with you. You won't ever become all you were created to be if you're against yourself. You have to retrain your mind. Be disciplined about what you dwell on.

TODAY'S PRAYER

Father, You have promised to take the scars of my
life and turn them into stars, to give me beauty for ashes,
and to pay me back double for anything lost. I believe that
You restore health and give new opportunities and
new relationships and new perspectives. Amen.

TODAY'S THOUGHT

You may be in pain today, but don't sit around nursing
your wounds. Don't let bitterness and discouragement set the
tone for your life. God is saying, "Arise. Wipe away the tears
and change the channel." God is going to make the
rest of your life the best of your life.

Remember the Right Things

Scripture Reading: 1 Chronicles 16

Look to the LORD and his strength; seek his face always.
Remember the wonders he has done, his miracles, and the
judgments he pronounced, you his servants . . .
1 Chronicles 16:11–13

Several years ago, I was playing basketball with our son, Jonathan. We've played one-on-one for years. For the first time, he beat me, fair and square, 15–14. I gave him a high five. Then I told him he was grounded!

During the game, at one point Jonathan dribbled around me and went up for a shot. I came out of nowhere, timed it just right, and blocked his shot. I swatted the ball away and it went flying into the bushes. I felt like an NBA star.

A couple days later, we went to the gym to play with some friends. Jonathan said, "Dad, tell everybody what happened the other night."

I said, "Oh, yeah, Jonathan went up for this shot, and I must have been this high in the air and I blocked it. It was something else."

He said, "No, Dad. I meant tell them how I beat you for the first time!"

What's funny is, I didn't remember my defeat; I remembered my victory. The first thing that came to my mind wasn't that I lost the game to him, but the fact that I did something good. It's because I've trained my mind to remember the right things.

For many people it's just the opposite. They won the game, but they remember all the mistakes they made. They never feel good about themselves. They're always focused on something they didn't do good enough.

It's all in how you train your mind. It depends on what channel you're watching. Don't make the mistake of remembering what you should forget, whether it's your hurts, your disappointments, or your failures. Don't forget what you should remember—your victories, your successes, and the hard times you overcame.

TODAY'S PRAYER

Father God, thank You that You are just waiting to release healing, restoration, favor, promotion, and abundance. I want to remember what You've done in my life and learn to respond with three simple words, "Lord, I believe." I want to get into agreement with You and see the incredible greatness of Your power activated. Amen.

TODAY'S THOUGHT

If you've been negative for a long time, you will need to retrain your thinking from your hurts and failures to your victories and your successes. Don't let the good things God has done in your life slip away.

Collect the Positives in Your Past

Scripture Reading: Joshua 4

"Go over before the ark of the LORD your God into the middle of the Jordan. Each of you is to take up a stone on his shoulder . . . to serve as a sign among you. In the future, when your children ask you, 'What do these stones mean?' tell them . . . These stones are to be a memorial to the people of Israel forever."

Joshua 4:5–7

In the Old Testament, God commanded His people to have certain feasts and celebrations so they would remember what He had done. Several times a year they would stop what they were doing and celebrate how God brought them out of slavery, defeated their enemies, and protected them. They were required to remember.

In another place it talks about how they put down what they called "memorial stones." Today, we would call these big stones "historical markers." The stones reminded them of specific victories. Every time they would go by certain stones they would recall an event, such as when they crossed over the Jordan into the Promised Land. Having these memorial stones helped them to keep God's deeds fresh in their memories.

In the same way, you should have your own memorial stones. When you look back over your life, you should not be remembering what you're supposed to forget. You should remember when you met the love of your life, when your child was born, when you got that new position, and when the problem suddenly turned around. Remember the strength you had in that difficult time when you lost a loved one. It looked dark. You didn't think you'd see another happy day again, but God turned it around and gave you joy for mourning, beauty for ashes, and today you're happy, healthy, and strong.

My mother recently marked the thirty-first anniversary of her victory over cancer. Thirty-one years ago, the doctors gave her a few weeks to live, but another year just went by, and she's still healthy and whole. That's a memorial stone.

Another one for me is December 1, 2003, when Mayor Lee Brown handed us the key to our new church building in Houston. I'm constantly remembering the good things.

My question to you is: Do you have any memorial stones out? What you remember will have a great impact on what kind of life you live.

TODAY'S PRAYER
Father, I am at peace today because I can look back
on the memorial stones in my life and remember the victories
that You have accomplished. Thank You for that time when
all the odds were against me, but You turned it around.
I believe You're doing the same today. Amen.

TODAY'S THOUGHT
Even if you feel you are in your darkest hour,
boldly declare the favor of God in the past, and nothing
can keep you down. Keep on remembering, believing,
expecting, and declaring. You may not be able to see it right
now, but things are going to change.

Rehearse Your Victories

Scripture Reading: 1 Samuel 17

*"Your servant has killed both the lion and the bear;
this uncircumcised Philistine will be like one of them,
because he has defied the armies of the living God. The Lord
who rescued me from the paw of the lion and the paw of the
bear will rescue me from the hand of this Philistine."*

1 Samuel 17:36–37

If you would just change what you're remembering—start remembering your successes, your victories, and the times you've overcome—that will allow you to step into new levels of favor. You may be in tough times, facing challenges, but when you remember the right things, you won't be saying, "This problem is too big. This sickness is going to be the end of me." Instead, you'll be saying, "God, You did it for me once, and I know You can do it for me again."

This is what David did when he was about to face Goliath, a giant twice his size. He could have focused on how big Goliath was and how Goliath had more experience, more training, and more weapons. All that would have done is discourage him.

The Scripture says, "David remembered that he had killed a lion and a bear with his own hands." What was he doing? Remembering his victories. David could have remembered that his brothers mistreated him and his father disrespected him. There were negative things in his past, just like with all of us. But David understood this principle: Dwelling on defeats, failures, and unfair situations will keep you stuck.

He chose to dwell on his victories, and he rose above that challenge and became who God created him to be. You may feel like you're up against a giant. The way you're going to stay encouraged and the way you will have the faith to overcome is to do as David did.

Instead of dwelling on how impossible it is and how you'll never make it, remember your victories all through the day. Get your memorial stones out. "Lord, thank You for that time when all the odds were against me, but You turned it around. God, I remember when You promoted me, vindicated me, made my wrongs right."

Rehearse your victories. Remembering the good things will make you strong.

TODAY'S PRAYER

Father, thank You that I am Your child, anointed, equipped, and well able to overcome. I am not weak, defeated, or powerless. I will not be intimidated, shrink back and think my problems are too big. You are greater than anything that is against me, and You control my destiny. Amen.

TODAY'S THOUGHT

If you are facing a giant challenge, don't focus on the size of the problem; focus on the size of your God. He's brought you through with victories in the past, and He will bring you through in the future.

Relive the Joy

Scripture Reading: Isaiah 63

I will tell of the kindnesses of the LORD, the deeds for which he is to be praised, according to all the LORD has done for us—yes, the many good things he has done for Israel, according to his compassion and many kindnesses.

Isaiah 63:7

In 2007, a young lady named Rachel Smith won the Miss USA beauty pageant. She's a very bright girl who has traveled the world helping underprivileged children. Later that year, she competed in the Miss Universe pageant. As she was walking out on the stage, during the evening gown competition, she lost her footing on the slick floor and fell flat on her back. Millions of people around the world were watching on television. She was so embarrassed. She got up as quickly as she could and kept a smile on her face. The audience wasn't very forgiving. There were jeers and laughs and boos. It was very humiliating.

In spite of that fall, Rachel made it to the top five. She had to go up and answer a question randomly chosen from a hat. She walked out again to the same spot where she had fallen just a few minutes early. She pulled a question out of the hat with millions of people watching. The question was: "If you could relive and redo any moment of your life over again, what moment would that be?"

She had just experienced the most embarrassing moment of her life twenty minutes earlier. How many of us would have said, "I'd like to relive that moment when I fell on this stage. I'd like to do that over again."

But without missing a beat she said, "If I could relive anything again, I would relive my trip to Africa working with the orphans, seeing their beautiful smiles, feeling their warm hugs." Instead of reliving a moment of embarrassment, a moment of pain, Rachel chose to replay a moment of joy, where she was making a difference, where she was proud of herself.

We all fall down in our lives. We all make mistakes. We all have embarrassing, unfair moments. You can be sure those images will replay again and again on the movie screen of your mind. You've got to do as Rachel Smith did: Change the channel and put on your victories, put on your successes, put on your accomplishments.

TODAY'S PRAYER

Father God, I believe that when negative memories come up that I have the power to change to the joy channel and be strong in the power of Your great might. I believe You will not only bring me out, but You will bring me out better off than I was before! Amen.

TODAY'S THOUGHT

Praise God for everything that happens to you, for He can turn it into a blessing. Put your shoulders back and hold your head up high. Walk as a child of the Most High God.

God Can Do It Again

Scripture Reading: Psalm 78

They forgot what he had done, the wonders he had shown them.
He did miracles in the sight of their ancestors in the
land of Egypt, in the region of Zoan.
Psalm 78:11–12

God performed miracle after miracle for the Israelites. He supernaturally brought them out of slavery. He sent plagues upon their enemies. When they came to a dead end at the Red Sea, with Pharaoh and his army chasing them, it looked like their lives were all over, but the water parted. They went through the sea on dry ground. God gave them water out of a rock and led them by the cloud by day and the pillar of fire by night. But in spite of all of this, they never made it into the Promised Land.

Psalm 78 tells why. It says, "They forgot what God had done. They didn't remember His amazing miracles." When you forget what you should be remembering, it can keep you out of your Promised Land. The Israelites became discouraged, started complaining, and asked Moses, "Why did you bring us out here to die in the desert?" When they faced an enemy, they thought, "We don't have a chance." They already had seen God's goodness in amazing ways. They had seen God do the impossible, but because they forgot about it, they were afraid, worried, and negative. It kept them from their destiny.

Are you forgetting what God has done for you? Have you let what once was a miracle become ordinary? It doesn't excite you anymore. You don't thank God for it. Look back over your life and remember that God brought you to where you are, big things and small things. You'll know if God did it for you once, He can do it for you again.

You may get discouraged and think, "I don't see how I'll ever get out of this problem." But when that happens, go back and remember the Red Seas that God has parted for you. Every one of us can look back and see the hand of God on our lives. God has opened doors that should have never opened for you, just as He did for the Israelites. He's helped you accomplish things you never could have accomplished on your own. He's brought you out of difficulties that you thought you'd never survive. He's protected, promoted, and given you opportunity.

TODAY'S PRAYER

Father, thank You for all the amazing things You've done in my life, for the victories You've helped me win, for the restoration, the vindication, and the favor You've shown. Help me to remember the doors You've opened for me and for the times You've protected, promoted, and given me opportunities. Amen.

TODAY'S THOUGHT

Remember that God brought you to where you are, big things and small things. Dwell on the fact that Almighty God has been and is on your side. Stand on the fact that He's promised to fight your battles for you. He can do it again.

Go Forth to Conquer

Scripture Reading: Exodus 14

Hear this, . . . all who live in the land. Has anything like this
ever happened in your days or in the days of your ancestors?
Tell it to your children, and let your children tell it to their
children, and their children to the next generation.

Joel 1:2–3

The key to staying encouraged so you can see God open new doors and turn negative situations around is to never forget what He has done. In fact, the Scripture says, "We should tell our children and our grandchildren." We should pass down stories of the goodness of God.

In the Old Testament, we read a lot about the staffs people carried around with them. They weren't just walking sticks, or something to keep wild animals away. They were more significant than that.

Back in those days, people were nomadic. They were always on the move. They didn't keep records with papers and computer files like we have today. Instead, they etched records of important events and dates on their walking staffs. That was their way of keeping personal records. They'd etch notations such as, "On this date God brought us out of slavery. On this date God gave us water out of the rock."

Their walking staffs provided a record of their history with God. When Moses parted the Red Sea, what did he do? He held up his staff (Exodus 14:16). He was saying, "God, we thank You for all You've done in the past. We remember that You've delivered us time and time again." Moses was remembering the great things God had done.

When David went out to face Goliath, he didn't just take his slingshot. The Scripture says he took his staff. On that staff, no doubt, he had etched, "On this date I killed a lion with my bare hands. On this date I killed a bear. On this date Samuel anointed me as king." David took his staff to remind him that God had helped him in the past. I can imagine just before he went out to fight, he ran over and read it one more time. That gave him the final boost. His attitude was, "God, You did it for me back then, so I know You can do it for me now."

Read the victories etched on your staff and go forth to conquer.

TODAY'S PRAYER

Father, thank You for Your goodness, protection, provisions, and favor. You've been awesome in my life and I thank You for it. I believe that no matter what I face today that You can do the miracles again for me now just as You've done in the past. Amen.

TODAY'S THOUGHT

When you remember and believe, you have the Creator of the universe fighting your battles, arranging things in your favor, going before you, moving the wrong people out of the way. I believe and declare you are going to see God's goodness in amazing ways!

Expect Greater Victories

Scripture Reading: Psalm 77

Then I thought, "To this I will appeal: the years
when the Most High stretched out his right hand.
I will remember the deeds of the LORD; yes, I will remember
your miracles of long ago. I will consider all your
works and meditate on all your mighty deeds."

Psalm 77:10–12

Are you facing giants today? Does your problem look too big? Do your dreams seem impossible? You need to get your staff out. Instead of going around discouraged and thinking it's never going to work out, start dwelling on your victories. Start thinking about how you killed the lion and bear in your own life. Start remembering how far God has brought you.

Rehearse all the times He opened doors, gave you promotions, healed your family members, and put you in the right places with the right people. Don't forget your victories. On a regular basis go back over your memorial stones and read the victories etched on your staff.

When those negative memories come up, they come to all of us—the things that didn't work out, your hurts, your failures, and your disappointments. Many people mistakenly stay on that channel and they end up stuck in a negative rut and do not expect anything good. Remember, that's not the only channel—get your remote control and switch over to the victory channel.

Expect breakthroughs. Expect problems to turn around. Expect to rise to new levels. You haven't seen your greatest victories. You haven't accomplished your greatest dreams. There are new mountains to climb and new horizons to explore.

Don't let past disappointments steal your passion. Don't let the way somebody treated you sour you on life. God is still in control. It may not have happened in the past, but it can happen in the future.

Draw a line in the sand and say, "That's it. I'm done with low expectations. I'm not settling for mediocrity. I expect favor, increase, and promotion. I expect blessings to chase me down. I expect this year to be my best year so far."

TODAY'S PRAYER

Father in Heaven, You see the challenges in my life and where the odds are stacked high against me. There are giants in front of me, but I'm not worried about them. I remember Your great deeds and miracles in my life, and I believe I will see greater victories than I've ever seen. Amen.

TODAY'S THOUGHT

If you raise your level of expectancy, God will take you places you've never dreamed. He'll open doors no man can shut. He will help you overcome obstacles that looked insurmountable, and you will see His goodness in amazing ways.

Have a
POSITIVE
Mind-set

Choose a Good Attitude

Scripture Reading: 1 John 5

. . . for everyone born of God overcomes the world.
This is the victory that has overcome the world, even our faith.
Who is it that overcomes the world? Only the one who
believes that Jesus is the Son of God.

1 John 5:4–5

Every day we get to choose our attitudes. We can determine to be happy and look on the bright side—expecting good things and believing we will accomplish our dreams—or we can elect to be negative by focusing on our problems, dwelling on what didn't work out, and living worried and discouraged.

These are the choices we all can make. Nobody can force you to have a certain attitude. Life will go so much better if you simply decide to be positive. When you wake up, choose to be happy. That is the fourth undeniable quality of a winner.

Choose to be grateful for the day. Choose to look on the bright side. Choose to focus on the possibilities. A good attitude does not automatically come. If you don't choose it, then more than likely you'll default to a negative mind-set, thinking: "I don't feel like going to work. I've got so many obstacles. Nothing good is in my future."

A negative attitude will limit your life. We all face difficulties. We all have tough times, but the right attitude is, "This is not permanent; it's only temporary. In the meantime I'm going to enjoy my life."

Maybe you didn't get the promotion you worked hard for, or you didn't qualify for that house you wanted. You could easily live with a sour attitude. Instead, you should think: "That's all right. I know something better is coming."

If you become caught in traffic, think positively: "I'm not going to be stressed. I know I'm at the right place at the right time."

If your medical report wasn't good, you can choose to think: "I'm not worried. This too shall pass."

If your dream is taking longer than you thought, you can choose to think: "I'm not discouraged. I know the right people and the right opportunities are already in my future, and at the right time it will come to pass."

TODAY'S PRAYER

Father, You have promised to give us the desires of our hearts. I have dreams in my heart that seem impossible. But You promised it, and now I choose to believe You for them, and I'm bold enough to ask You for them. I'm asking for Your favor to shine down on me. Amen.

TODAY'S THOUGHT

Stop dwelling on negative, destructive attitudes that keep you in a rut. Your life will change when you change your attitude. God has so much more in store for you. If you want to see God's far and beyond favor, you have to start believing it.

Set Your Mind to Positive

Rejoice in the Lord always. I will say it again: Rejoice! . . . The Lord is near. Do not be anxious about anything, but in every situation, by prayer and petition, with thanksgiving, present your requests to God. And the peace of God, which transcends all understanding, will guard your hearts and your minds in Christ Jesus.

Philippians 4:4–7

When you have a positive mind-set, you cannot be defeated. No matter what comes your way, you shake it off and keep moving ahead.

Life is like a car, with a forward and a reverse gear. You decide which way you want to go. It doesn't take any more effort to go forward than it does backward. If you choose to focus on the positive and keep your mind set on your possibilities, you will move forward and see increase and favor. But if you dwell on the negative and stay focused on problems and what you don't have, and how impossible your dream looks, that's just like putting your car in reverse—you'll go backward. It's all about what you choose to dwell on. You can choose to dwell on what's wrong with you or what's right with you.

There is good and bad in every situation. If you'll have the right attitude, you can always find the good. It's like this little boy I heard about. He had a baseball bat and a ball, and he said to himself, "I'm the best hitter in all the world."

He threw the ball up, swung, and missed: Strike one!

The boy picked up the ball, straightened his cap, and said it again: "I'm the best hitter in all the world."

He tossed the ball up and swung and missed again: Strike two!

This time he said it with even more determination: "I'm the best hitter in all the world!"

He tossed the ball up, swung away, and missed again. Strike three!

The boy then laid down the bat, smiled real big, and said, "What do you know? I'm the best pitcher in all the world."

Be like this boy and stay positive. That's a winner's mind-set. Learn to look on the bright side. Find the silver lining in every cloud.

TODAY'S PRAYER

Father God, You said all things are going to work together for my good. By faith in You, I am well able. I am equipped. I am empowered. My mind is filled with good thoughts, not thoughts of defeat. Thank You that You are faithful to Your Word and will work mightily in my behalf.

TODAY'S THOUGHT

When times get tough—as they often do—or things don't go your way—as they sometimes don't—keep on believing in God. Boldly remind yourself that God is opening doors of opportunity for you. Dare today to start believing God for greater things.

Know That God Is in Control

Scripture Reading: Genesis 39

But while Joseph was there in the prison, the LORD was with him; he showed him kindness and granted him favor in the eyes of the prison warden. So the warden . . . made [Joseph] responsible for all that was done there. . . . because the LORD was with Joseph and gave him success in whatever he did.

Genesis 39:20–23

A lot of people use the excuse, "I'm negative because I've had negative things happen to me." They'll offer excuses such as:

"My business didn't make it."

"A friend did me wrong."

"I had a bad childhood."

"I'm dealing with a sickness, and that's why I'm sour."

It's not your circumstances that make you negative; it's your attitude about those circumstances. You can take twenty positive people and twenty negative people and give them the exact same problem—put them on the same job, in the same family, and at the same house—and the twenty positive people will come out just as positive and happy, with great attitudes. The negative people will still be just as negative. They can have the same problems and same circumstances, but much different attitudes.

What's the difference? Positive people have made up their minds to enjoy life. They focus on the possibility, not the problem. They're grateful for what they have, and they don't complain about what they don't have. Positive people know that God is in control, and that nothing happens without His permission. They choose to bloom where they are planted. They're not waiting to be happy when the situation changes. They're happy while God is changing the situation.

When you're positive, you're passing the test. You're saying, "God, I trust You. I know You're fighting my battles."

If you are not happy where you are, you won't get where you want to be. Don't wait for everything to change before you have a good attitude. If you have a good attitude now, God can change the situation.

TODAY'S PRAYER

Father, thank You that I can thrive and prosper, not just survive, despite every difficulty that may come my way. You've said that every setback is a setup for a comeback, therefore I will not give up my dreams or settle where I am. I believe one touch from You can change everything. Amen.

TODAY'S THOUGHT

You could see your whole life turn around if you'd simply start thinking thoughts that are consistent with the positive principles of God's Word. You must make a quality choice to keep your mind focused on the good things of God and experience His best for your life.

Keep the Right Perspective

Scripture Reading: Colossians 3

*And set your minds and keep them set on what is above
(the higher things), not on the things that are on the earth.*
Colossians 3:2 AMP

Some people would love to have your problems. They would gladly trade places with you. They would love to have the job that frustrates you. They would love to sit in traffic in that car you don't like. They would love to have your spouse, who gets on your nerves. They would love to live in the house you think is too small.

You may be thinking, "As soon as I get out of this neighborhood, I'm going to be happy." Instead, why don't you choose to be happy right where you are? Choose to have a good attitude without thinking about what you have or don't have.

Your happiness is all about your approach to life. One man gets up and says, "Good morning, Lord." Another man gets up and says, "Oh Lord, it's morning." Which person are you?

You control what kind of day you're having. You're as happy as you want to be. It's not your circumstances that keep you unhappy. It's how you respond to them.

A lot of times we're making ourselves unhappy. You can't change the traffic, the weather, or how others treat you. If your happiness is based on everything going your way and everybody treating you right, you will be frustrated.

Before you leave the house, you need to make up your mind to stay positive and enjoy the day no matter what comes your way. You have to decide ahead of time.

That's what it says in Colossians 3:2, "Set your mind on the higher things and keep it set." The higher things are the positive things. When you get out of bed in the morning, you need to set your mind for victory. Set your mind for success. Have the attitude: "This is going to be a great day. God's favor is on my life. I'm excited about my future."

When your mind is set as positive, hopeful, and expecting good things, that's when you'll go places you've never dreamed. New doors will open. New opportunities, and the right people will come across your path.

TODAY'S PRAYER

Father, thank You that You have crowned me with favor. I will not be limited by my past or present circumstances. I'm setting my mind on higher things, pressing forward and taking new ground, stretching my faith, believing for bigger things, expecting Your blessing in unprecedented ways. I believe that You are taking me places I've never dreamed. Amen.

TODAY'S THOUGHT

You can't start the day in neutral. You must continually choose, twenty-four hours a day, to keep your mind on the positive things of God, especially being on guard during times of adversity, in times of personal challenge.

Winning Is in Your DNA

Scripture Reading: 2 Corinthians 9

And God is able to bless you abundantly,
so that in all things at all times, having all that you need,
you will abound in every good work.
2 Corinthians 9:8

A lot of people live by Murphy's Law, which says, "If anything can go wrong, it will, and at the worst possible time. Things will take longer than you thought. It will be more difficult than it seems." If you have fallen into that mind-set, change your outlook.

You are a child of the Most High God. You've been crowned with favor. You were never created to live an average, get-by, short-end-of-the-stick life. You were created to be the head and not the tail, to lend and not borrow, to reign in life as a king. You have royalty in your blood. Winning is in your DNA.

Now get rid of that negative mentality, and set your mind for victory, for increase, and for good breaks. Start expecting your plans to work out and for people to be good to you. If it doesn't happen, don't fall back into that old negative mentality by thinking things like: "I should have known it would not work out for me. I never get good breaks."

You are not a victim. You're a victor. You wouldn't have opposition if there were not something amazing in your future. Keep a smile on your face. Keep a spring in your step. Stay positive. Stay hopeful. God is still on the throne.

Being sour, negative, and pessimistic, and expecting the worst will keep you from your destiny. You may have had a lot of negative, unfair things happen in your past, but don't let that become a stronghold. Don't live with that negative mentality.

If God showed you all He has planned for you, it would boggle your mind. If you could see the doors He's going to open, the opportunities that will cross your path, and the people who will show up, you'd be so amazed, excited, and passionate, it would be easy to set your mind for victory.

This is what faith is all about. You have to believe it before you see it. God's favor is surrounding you like a shield. Every setback is a setup for a comeback. Every bad break, every disappointment, and every person who does you wrong is part of the plan to get you to where you're supposed to be.

TODAY'S PRAYER

Father, thank You that because I am Your child, and
You are the Most High God, I have royalty in my blood.
You are still on the throne, and I can't wait to see the doors
You are going to open up and the opportunities that will
cross my path in the future. Amen.

TODAY'S THOUGHT

Don't fall into the trap of being negative, complacent,
or just taking whatever life brings your way. Set the tone for
victory, for success, for new levels. Enlarge your vision. Make
room for God to do something new. You haven't touched
the surface of what He has in store.

Get Your Hopes Up

Scripture Reading: Ephesians 1

I pray that your hearts will be flooded with light so that you can understand the confident hope he has given to those he called— his holy people who are his rich and glorious inheritance.

Ephesians 1:18 NLT

I was talking to a reporter one time, and I could tell he didn't like the fact that my message is so positive and so hopeful. He asked what I would tell a person who lost a job and was about to lose a home and had no place to go and all sorts of other problems. He painted the worst possible situation.

I said, "First of all, I would encourage that person to get up and find something to be grateful for; and secondly, I would encourage the person to expect things to turn around, expect new doors to open, expect breakthroughs."

The Scripture says, "When darkness overtakes the righteous, light will come bursting in." When you don't see a way out, and it's dark, you're in prime position for God's favor to come bursting in.

The reporter said, "Wouldn't that be giving them false hope?"

Here's the alternative: I could tell them be negative, bitter, give up, complain, and be depressed. All that would do is make matters worse.

You may be in a difficult situation, but instead of being negative just dig in your heels and say, "I refuse to live with a negative attitude. I'm not giving up on my dreams. I'm not living without passion or zeal. I may not see a way, but I know God has a way. It may be dark, but I'm expecting the light to come bursting in. I'm setting my mind for victory."

That's what allows God to work. It's not just mind over matter. It's not just having a positive attitude. It's your faith being released. When you believe, it gets God's attention. When you expect your dreams to come to pass, your health restored, and good breaks and divine connections coming your way, then the Creator of the universe goes to work.

TODAY'S PRAYER

Father, thank You for unveiling Your great heart of love and grace that brings me hope. Thank You that when I don't see the way out, and it's dark, that You come bursting in with light and direction. I release my faith that You, the Creator of the universe, have highly favored me. Amen.

TODAY'S THOUGHT

Friend, you must get your hopes up, or you won't have faith. You don't have to figure out how God is going to solve your problems or bring it to pass. That's His responsibility. Your job is to believe. Your faith will help you overcome your obstacles.

Get in the Flow of God's Favor

Scripture Reading: Isaiah 40

. . . but those who hope in the Lord will renew their strength.
They will soar on wings like eagles; they will run and
not grow weary, they will walk and not be faint.

Isaiah 40:31

You may have had a thousand bad breaks, but don't use that as an excuse to be negative. One good break can make up for all the bad breaks. One touch of God's favor can catapult you further than you ever imagined. You may feel like you're getting behind. You're not where you thought you would be in life. Don't worry; God knows how to make up for lost time. He knows how to accelerate things.

Now you must do your part. Shake off a negative mentality. Shake off pessimism, discouragement, and self-pity. Get your fire back. Life is passing you by. You don't have time to waste being negative. You have a destiny to fulfill. You have an assignment to accomplish. What's in your future is greater than anything you've seen in your past. We need to get rid of Murphy's Law and live by just the opposite. Your attitude should be: "If anything can go right today, it will go right and happen to me at the best time. Nothing will be as difficult as it looks. Nothing will take as long as it seems."

Why? You are highly favored. Almighty God is breathing in your direction. You've been anointed, equipped, and empowered.

Some may claim I'm just getting hopes up and trying to

get people to be more positive. That is true, and here's why: God is a positive God. There is nothing negative about Him. If you're negative, sour, or pessimistic, you're going against the flow of God.

When we fly from Houston to Los Angeles, it takes thirty minutes longer to get there than it does to fly back, because the jet stream flows from west to east, slowing us down. The plane has to work harder, use more fuel, and expend more energy. But when we travel back home, it's just the opposite. The jet stream works in our favor, pushing us forward and making it easier, saving us time and energy.

The same principles apply in life. When you are positive, hopeful, and expecting good things, you are in the jet stream of almighty God. Things will be easier. You will accomplish more, live happier, and see increase and favor.

TODAY'S PRAYER

Father, thank You that You are accelerating Your plan in my life and that I am in the divine flow as I put my trust in you. I believe that You will accomplish my dreams faster than I thought possible, and that You have blessings that will thrust me forward years ahead. Amen.

TODAY'S THOUGHT

If you will take the limits off God, you will see Him do amazing things. Divine connections are coming your way. It will be bigger than you imagined. He will bring out gifts and talents you didn't even know you had. He will open up new doors of opportunity.

You Become What You Believe

Scripture Reading: Matthew 9 MSG

As Jesus left the house, he was followed by two blind men crying out, "Mercy, Son of David! Mercy on us!" When Jesus got home, the blind men went in with him. Jesus said to them, "Do you really believe I can do this?" They said, "Why, yes, Master!" He touched their eyes and said, "Become what you believe." It happened. They saw.

Matthew 9:27–30 MSG

You can't think negative thoughts and live a positive life. When you think, "I'll never pass this chemistry test. I dread going to work. My marriage will not last. I'll never meet the right person," that's going against the flow. Your life follows your thoughts. You're drawing in what you're thinking about, just like a magnet.

"I can't pass this test." You're drawing in defeat.

"I can't stand going to work." You're drawing in negativity.

"I'll never meet the right person." You're drawing in loneliness.

"I'll never accomplish my dreams." You're drawing in mediocrity.

I read a study done on people who needed arthroscopic knee surgery. Their knees were worn down and they needed the joint to be cleaned out. On some of the patients, the doctors received family permission to only pretend to do the surgery as part of this study. Instead of actually cleaning out the knee and performing the full surgery, they simply put the patient under anesthesia and made three tiny incisions around the knee as if they had done something.

When those patients woke up, they thought their surgery had been performed. It's interesting that after two years, the patients who'd had the fake surgery reported just as much relief from the pain as the patients who'd actually had the surgery.

You may think that the patients who did not get the surgery were feeling no pain because their minds had been tricked. That wasn't the case. When the doctors examined their knees over time, they could see improvements, even without the surgery. Their conclusion was that when the brain expected the knee to get better, it did, even without surgery. Just thinking that the knee was healed actually helped the body to heal.

TODAY'S PRAYER

Father, thank You that I can magnify You as high and lifted up above any doubt, fear, anxiety, or negativity. Whatever the problem or difficulty is, You are greater. I placed my faith in You, and I believe that my life will follow my thoughts, just like a magnet. Amen.

TODAY'S THOUGHT

What are you believing? Are you believing to go higher in life, to rise above your obstacles, to live in health, abundance, healing, and victory? As was true of the blind men who received their sight, you will become what you believe.

Guard Your Heart and Mind

Scripture Reading: Proverbs 4

Above all else, guard your heart,
for everything you do flows from it.
Proverbs 4:23

How many people go through the day feeling unqualified, inferior, and insecure? Their brains say, "I've got my instructions. Let me perform what they're asking. I've got to make sure they're clumsy and slow and don't have any good ideas." What's the problem? They have programmed themselves for defeat. Their minds are working just perfectly.

The good news is this also works in the right direction. When you go through the day saying, "I'm equipped, I'm empowered, and I am well able," your brain goes to work saying, "Let's make sure this person is at the top of the game, skilled, intelligent, creative, confident, and secure."

You may be facing a sickness, but you should not say, "I'll never get well." Instead, say, "I'm getting better and better. Health and healing are flowing through me. God is renewing my youth." The brain goes to work saying to your whole system: "Do you hear what she's saying? She says she's healthy. She's whole. She's strong. Get busy and release the healing. Create new cells. Unleash strength, energy, and vitality."

Maybe you struggle with an addiction. Don't ever say, "I'll never overcome it. I'm just hooked." If you believe you're an addict, you'll always be an addict.

When you dwell on negative, defeated thoughts, you poison your system. You are telling your mind—this incredible tool God has given you—to release defeat, failure, and mediocrity. That's why the Scripture says you have to guard your heart and mind.

If you're trying to lose weight, don't ever say, "I'll never lose this weight. I'm so undisciplined. My metabolism is so messed up, even if I worked out all day it wouldn't make a difference." When you do that your mind tells your system, "Stay messed up. Keep every calorie you can. Send out new cravings. Take away the desire to exercise. Make sure they feel bad, deplete all their energy."

When you get up in the morning, no matter how you feel, say to yourself, "I'm getting thinner. This weight is coming off. I'm strong, healthy, and energetic. I have discipline and self-control. I look good. I feel good. I think good."

TODAY'S PRAYER

Father, thank You that my mind can be reprogrammed to thoughts of health and renewal and abundance and self-control. Thank You that I can be free from the poison of negativity. I believe that as I guard my heart and mind with truth that You will unleash strength in my life. Amen.

TODAY'S THOUGHT

When you align your thoughts with God's thoughts and start dwelling on the promises of His Word, when you constantly dwell on thoughts of His victory and favor, you will be propelled toward greatness, inevitably bound for increase, promotion, and God's supernatural blessings.

Focus on the Positive

Scripture Reading: Psalm 1

But his delight is in the law of the LORD,
and in His law he meditates day and night.

Psalm 1:2 NKJV

Just because a thought comes into your mind doesn't mean you have to dwell on it. You control the doorway to your mind. If the thought is negative, discouraging, and pushing you down, dismiss it. Don't dwell on it. Keep the door closed. Choose to dwell on thoughts that empower you, inspire you, and encourage you to have faith, hope, and joy.

If you keep your mind filled with the right thoughts, there won't be any room for the wrong thoughts. All through the day you should be focused on the positive: "Something good is going to happen to me. I'm strong, healthy, talented, and disciplined. I can do all things through Christ. My best days are still out in front of me." When your mind is filled with thoughts of faith, hope, and victory, you will draw in the good things of God.

I read about a lady who had been sick for several years. She tried different doctors, but they couldn't figure out what was wrong. She was very negative, always talking about how she would never get well. Like a magnet, she kept drawing in more sickness. Then she went to another doctor and complained on and on and told him she would never get well. The doctor noticed her negative attitude and gave her an unusual prescription. He'd never done this before. He said, "Every hour that you're awake, I want you to say at least six times, 'I'm getting better and better every day in every way.'"

She said, "Doctor, I'm not going to do that. I want some real medicine."

"No, you follow my orders, and then we'll talk about what's next," he said.

The patient started doing this fifty to sixty times a day, and before long her attitude began to change. Within a few days, she was feeling better. A couple of weeks later, her strength returned, and then her joy was back. A month later, she was a different person. All the symptoms were gone. She went back to the doctor. He looked at the report on her blood work and said everything was perfectly normal.

The real battle takes place in your mind. You attract what you're dwelling on all day.

TODAY'S PRAYER

Father, thank You that because You are in control of my life, I can stay full of hope, knowing that You are fighting my battles for me. Your thoughts fill me with faith, hope, and victory. I believe that You are always at my side, and that no weapon formed against me shall prosper. Amen.

TODAY'S THOUGHT

Engage your mind in thoughts of joy, peace, victory, abundance, and blessings, and you will move toward those things, drawing them to yourself at the same time. If you choose to stay focused on the positive and keep your mind set on the good things of God, all the forces of darkness are not going to be able to keep you from moving forward and fulfilling your destiny.

Freshen Up Your Attitude

Scripture Reading: Ephesians 4

*And be constantly renewed in the spirit of your mind
[having a fresh mental and spiritual attitude] . . .*
Ephesians 4:23 AMP

Sometimes your body will not get well until your mind tells it to get well. You won't accomplish your dreams by thinking, "I never get any good breaks. I don't know the right people. I don't have the funds or the education." You have to give yourself permission to accomplish your dreams, permission to get out of debt, and permission to overcome the obstacle. Your better days begin in your thinking.

Studies show that when you are negative and think sad, discouraging thoughts, your serotonin level goes down, and that causes you to feel sad. It's not just in your head. It affects your moods. But when you get up each day in a positive frame of mind, feeling hopeful and expecting good things, endorphins are released that make you feel happy. You will have more energy, because being positive puts a spring in your step.

If you go around with negative thoughts, they will drain you of your energy and zeal. It's like a big vacuum pulling out all the good things that God put in you. You'd be amazed at how much better you'd feel and how much more you'd accomplish if you'd just switch over to this positive mind-set. You have to think positive thoughts on purpose. "This is going to be a great day. This is my year. I'm expecting an abundance of favor."

The Scripture says, "Put on a fresh new attitude." I've found yesterday's attitude is not good enough for today. Every morning you have to consciously adopt a fresh attitude by thinking things like: "I'm going to be happy today. I'm going to be good to people. I'm going to go with the flow and not get upset. God is in control. He's directing my steps. No obstacle is too big. I am well able to do what I'm called to do."

That fresh new attitude will put you in God's jet stream. You will accomplish things that you could not accomplish on your own. You'll be more productive. You'll have more wisdom, creativity, and good ideas. You will overcome obstacles that were bigger, stronger, and more powerful.

TODAY'S PRAYER

Father, thank You that I can enter into the flow
of positive, faith-filled thoughts of victory. I choose to
start seeing the best in situations. I believe that as I dwell
on Your Word that my mind will be renewed and
my life will be transformed. Amen.

TODAY'S THOUGHT

When you put on a fresh new attitude of faith,
you are opening the door for God to work in your situation.
You may not see anything happening with your natural eyes,
but in the spiritual world, God is at work. And if you'll
do your part and keep believing, at the right time,
God will bring you out with the victory.

Live in a Positive Mind-set

Scripture Reading: Daniel 6

I have strength for all things in Christ Who empowers me
[I am ready for anything and equal to anything through
Him Who infuses inner strength into me; I am
self-sufficient in Christ's sufficiency].

Philippians 4:13 AMP

A lot of people rely on yesterday's attitude, or last week's attitude, or last year's attitude. That thing is old and stale. Start putting on a fresh new attitude, every morning. Get your mind going in the right direction. Develop the habit of living in a positive mind-set.

This is what the Bible's Daniel did. The Scripture says he had an excellent spirit. He was a cut above. He stood out in the crowd. Every morning he got up early, opened his window, and thanked God for the day and for His goodness. He was putting on that fresh new attitude, setting his mind for victory.

Daniel was serving the king in a foreign land, when the king issued a decree that no one could pray to any God except the king's God. If they did, they would be thrown into a lions' den. That threat didn't stop Daniel. He kept praying to Jehovah.

Daniel's enemies told the king, who loved Daniel, but he couldn't go back on his word. Daniel said, "Don't worry, King. I'm going to be fine. The God I serve is well able to deliver me." The authorities threw Daniel into the lions' den. Everyone expected Daniel to be eaten in a few minutes. But when you have this attitude of faith, God will fight your battles for you. He sent an angel to close the mouths of the lions. The king came by the next morning, and Daniel was untouched. The king got him out and said, "From now on we're going to all worship the God of Daniel, the true and living God."

That's what happens when you start the day off in faith, thinking positive thoughts on purpose. When you're in a difficult situation, you don't shrink back in fear with thoughts like: "Why is this happening to me?" Instead, you rise up in faith and say, "My God is well able. I'm armed with strength for this battle. I can do all things through Christ."

My challenge today is for you to keep your mind going in the right direction. When you're positive, you are in the jet stream of God. Learn to think thoughts on purpose: "This will be a great day. Something good is going to happen to me."

TODAY'S PRAYER

Father, thank You that I can do all things through
Christ who infuses inner strength into me. You said I am
more than a conqueror, a victor and not a victim. Thank You
that today I can put on a fresh attitude that expects
the abundance of Your favor. Amen.

TODAY'S THOUGHT

The same God who kept Daniel safe in the lions' den
has put a hedge of protection around you. Whether you
realize it or not, you are lion proof. You are coming out
stronger, increased, and promoted just like Daniel.
God is even in control of your enemies.

Start Off Your Day in Faith

Scripture Reading: Daniel 1

"When you pass through the waters,
I will be with you; and when you pass through the rivers,
they will not sweep over you. When you walk through the fire,
you will not be burned; the flames will not set you ablaze.
For I am the LORD your God . . ."

Isaiah 43:2–3

It's interesting that the Scripture says nothing negative about either Joseph or Daniel. I'm sure they made mistakes, but you can't find a record of anything they did wrong. There are stories of other great heroes of faith such as Abraham, David, Moses, Paul, and Peter failing and making mistakes.

Daniel and Joseph were good people who experienced a long list of unfair things and bad circumstances. They were mistreated and faced huge obstacles. But if you study their lives, you'll find one common denominator: They were always positive. They had this attitude of faith. They started off each day with their minds going in the right direction, knowing that our God is well able. They both saw favor and blessings in amazing ways. In the same way, you can be a good person and have bad circumstances.

It's easy to get negative and say, "I don't understand why my child got off course. Why did I come down with this sickness? Why did these people do me wrong?" Instead, do as Daniel did. Get up every morning, look up and say, "Lord, thank You for another great day. You are well able, bigger than my problem, greater than this sickness, and more powerful than my enemy. Thank You that today things will change in my favor."

Especially in difficult times, make sure you put on this fresh new attitude. Set your mind for victory and keep it set. When negative thoughts come, dismiss them and make a declaration like Daniel's: "My God is well able. He's done it for me in the past, and I know He'll do it for me again in the future."

Start off your day in faith. If you develop this positive mind-set, you'll not only be happier, healthier, and stronger, but also, I believe and declare, you will accomplish more than you ever imagined. You will overcome obstacles that looked impossible, and you will become everything God has created you to be. You can, you will!

TODAY'S PRAYER

Father, thank You that today things will change in my favor. I know You are well able, bigger than my problem, greater than any sickness, and more powerful than any enemy. I believe that You will help me overcome every obstacle. Through Your strength, I can and I will. Amen.

TODAY'S THOUGHT

Both Joseph and Daniel experienced injustice, heartache, and pain because of somebody else's poor choices and bad attitude. Because they kept the right attitude, God brought them out much better than they were before. When somebody is mistreating you, or you're having financial difficulty, or your whole world is falling apart, expect God's favor to show up.

Commit to
EXCELLENCE

A Commitment to Excellence

Scripture Reading: Ezra 7

Whatever you do, work at it with all your heart,
as working for the Lord, not for human masters, since
you know that you will receive an inheritance from the Lord
as a reward. It is the Lord Christ you are serving.
Colossians 3:23–24

We live in a society in which mediocrity is the norm. Many people do as little as they can to get by. They don't take pride in their work or in who they are. If someone is watching, they may perform one way, but when nobody is watching, they cut corners and take the easy way out. If you are not careful, you can be pulled into this same mentality where you think it's okay to show up late to work, to look and to give less than your best.

But God doesn't bless mediocrity. God blesses excellence. I have observed that the fifth undeniable quality of a winner is a commitment to excellence. When you have a spirit of excellence, you do your best whether anyone is watching or not. You go the extra mile. You do more than you have to.

Other people may complain about their jobs and go around looking sloppy and cutting corners. Don't sink to that level. Everyone else may be slacking off at work, compromising in school, letting their lawns go, but here's the key: You are not everyone else. You are called to excellence. God wants you to set the highest standard.

You should be the model employee for your company.

Your boss and supervisors should be able to say to the new hires, "Watch him. Learn from her. Pick up the same habits. Develop the same skills. This person is the cream of the crop, always on time, has a great attitude and does more than what is required."

When you have an excellent spirit like that, you will not only see promotion and increase but you are honoring God. Some people think, "Let me read my Bible and go to church to honor God." And yes, that's true, but it honors God just as much to get to work on time, to be productive, and to look good each day. Your life gives praise to God.

Some people never go to church or listen to a sermon or read the Bible. Instead, they're reading your life. They're watching how you live. Make sure you look and live the best you possibly can. You're representing almighty God.

TODAY'S PRAYER

Father, thank You for calling me to live a life that honors You and for the privilege of representing You, the almighty God, to my loved ones and friends, my coworkers and neighbors and strangers. You have called me to excellence.
Help me to be the best I can be. Amen.

TODAY'S THOUGHT

You may be in a situation today where everybody around you is compromising their integrity or taking the easy way out. Don't go there. Be the one to have an excellent spirit. Do your work well and live in such a manner that when people see you, they are attracted to your God.

Exceed Expectations

Scripture Reading: Matthew 5

*"If anyone forces you to go one mile,
go with them two miles."*
Matthew 5:41

When you go to work, you should be so full of excellence that other people want what you have. Don't slack off, and don't give a halfhearted effort. Give it your all. Do your job to the best of your ability.

When you're a person of excellence, you do more than necessary. You don't just meet the minimum requirements; you go the extra mile. That phrase comes from the Bible. Jesus said, "If a soldier demands you carry his gear one mile, carry it two miles." In those days Roman soldiers were permitted by law to require someone else to carry their armor.

Jesus said, "Do more than is expected; carry it two miles." That's the attitude you need to have: "I'm not doing just what I have to. I'm not doing the minimum amount to keep my job. I'm a person of excellence. I go above and beyond what's asked of me. I do more than is expected."

This means if you're supposed to be at work at 8 a.m., you show up ten minutes early. You produce more than you have to. You stay ten minutes late. You don't start shutting down thirty minutes before closing. You put in a full day.

Many people show up to work fifteen minutes late. They get some coffee, wander around the office, and finally sit down to work a half hour late. They'll waste another half hour making personal phone calls and surfing the Internet. Then they wonder why they aren't promoted. It's because God doesn't reward sloppiness. God rewards excellence.

TODAY'S PRAYER

Father, I want to be a person of excellence in everything I do, to go the second mile and always be my best, and I want that excellence to flow out of my heart of love for You. I believe that as I give it my all that I will see Your goodness and favor in my life in new ways. Amen.

TODAY'S THOUGHT

Subtle compromises of excellence will keep us from God's best. Start making the more excellent choices in every area of life, even in mundane matters such as paying your bills on time. In everything you do, attempt to represent God well.

God Rewards Excellence

Scripture Reading: Genesis 24

After she had given him a drink, she said, "I'll draw water for your camels too, until they have had enough to drink." So she quickly emptied her jar into the trough, ran back to the well to draw more water, and drew enough for all his camels.

Genesis 24:19–20

In the Old Testament, Abraham sent his servant to a foreign country to find a wife for his son, Isaac. Abraham's servant prayed that he would know he'd found the right lady if she offered a drink to both him and his camels. The servant reached the city around sunset. A beautiful young lady named Rebekah came out to the well. The servant said, "I'm so thirsty. Would you mind lowering your bucket and getting me a drink?"

She said, "Not only that, let me get some water for your camels as well."

Here's what's interesting: After a long day's walk, a camel can drink thirty gallons of water. This servant had ten camels with him. Think about what Rebekah did. If she had a one-gallon bucket of water, she said, in effect, "Yes, I'll not only do what you asked and give you a drink, but I'll also dip down in this well three hundred more times and give your ten camels a drink."

Rebekah went way beyond the call of duty. As a result, she was chosen to marry Isaac, who came from the wealthiest family of that time. I doubt that she ever again had to draw three hundred gallons of water.

God rewards excellence. When you do more than what's required, you will see God's goodness in new ways.

You may be declaring favor and promotion over your life and that's all good, but it's only one part. The second part is making sure you get to work on time, do more than what's required, and do better this year than last year.

TODAY'S PRAYER

Father in Heaven, thank You that You are watching my life and that You reward excellence. I want to live this day to please You in everything, and I want to step up to a higher level of integrity and honesty in my relationships with other people. Help me to do what I know in my heart are the right things to do. Amen.

TODAY'S THOUGHT

God doesn't reward mediocrity; He blesses excellence. If you're stuck in a rut while others are being blessed and continuing to prosper and get ahead, consider whether the problem is one of your own making. Are you a person of excellence and integrity?

Strive for Excellence

Scripture Reading: Luke 19

"Well done, my good servant!" his master replied. "Because you have been trustworthy in a very small matter, take charge of ten cities."

Luke 19:17

We're in a very competitive marketplace. If you're not growing, improving, and learning new skills, you're falling behind.

On Sunday afternoons after our final church service, I sit down with a video editor and edit my own sermons. I've done over 625 messages in fifteen years. I study each one to see what could be better. I'll see that one point took a little too long to develop, or that another section of the speech was really great. Maybe I'll see that I'm talking a little fast or that I need to look out at one side of the audience more. I'm constantly evaluating and analyzing not only my speaking performance, but also the production, the lighting, and the camera angles. My attitude is that there's always room for improvement.

People watching on television will sometimes say, "Joel, I never hear you stutter or make a mistake." I always tell them it's because I know how to edit! I can fix every stutter, every pause. I don't have to, but I want my taped sermons to be the best they can possibly be. I don't want to be at the same level next year as I am now. I want to be more effective, more skilled, and making a greater impact.

When you're an excellent person, you don't get stagnant.

You're always taking steps to improve. Favor and being excellent go hand in hand. Increase, promotion, and reaching your highest potential are all tied to a spirit of excellence. Looking your best and taking care of your possessions are also part of this lifestyle.

Some people drive cars that haven't been washed in six months. They say that it's an old piece of junk and that they're planning on getting a better car. But if you don't take care of what God has given you, how can He bless you with more?

I've been in huts in Africa with dirt floors, but everything is clean, organized, perfectly in place. Why is that? The people have a spirit of excellence. Whether you have much or a little, whether it's old or new, take pride in what God has given you.

TODAY'S PRAYER

Father, thank You that creation is a reflection of Your amazing excellence and perfection in all that You do and in all that You are. Breathe Your Spirit into me so that I might be a trustworthy servant who reflects Your excellence in all that I do and in all that I am. I believe that as I am faithful to You, You will trust me with more. Amen.

TODAY'S THOUGHT

Take care of the resources God has given you. He will only trust us with more after we have been faithful with a little. Our lives are an open book before God. He looks at our hearts and motives. There's no limit to what God will do in your life when He knows that He can trust you.

Do It with Excellence

Scripture Reading: 1 Kings 6

Whatever your hand finds to do, do it with all your might . . .
Ecclesiastes 9:10

After services in our church, I usually walk up to the visitors' area to greet our guests. On the way, if I see a piece of paper or a gum wrapper on the floor, I pick it up. I don't have to do that. Somebody on our staff will get it eventually, but when you have a spirit of excellence, it's ingrained in you. To see any trash on the floor rubs me the wrong way.

Sometimes children from our nurseries drop crackers on the hallway floor. I always ask my assistant to call the cleaning crew if there is a big mess. I don't want people coming to the next service to see that on the floor. Why is that? It's not excellence if there is a mess on the floor. Our building represents almighty God. I have a responsibility to make sure it looks excellent. That's why we make sure the lawn looks perfect, the hallways are spotless, the equipment works, and the broadcast is exceptional.

Why? We represent God, and He is not sloppy. God is not run-down. God is not second-class. He is an excellent God.

It doesn't mean you must have the best to represent Him, but you should take care of what you have as best you can. Sometimes a can of paint can make all the difference in the world. Pulling some weeds, cleaning the carpet, getting more organized. Do what you can to represent God in an excellent way.

When our children were small, we took them to Disney-land. That place was spotless. I never once saw gum stuck to the floor. Hundreds of thousands of people go through every year, and the entire park looked brand-new. I thought, "How do they do it?" One day, I saw employees going around with tools that scrape up gum. That's what they do all day long.

If Disney can keep their parks that clean and that first-class, we should make God's house clean and first-class. Now apply the same standards to your own life, your house, your car, your clothes, your cubicle, and your office. I'm not talking about spending a lot of money. It's how you choose to take care of what God's given you. I'm asking you to do it with excellence.

TODAY'S PRAYER

Father, thank You that You have called me to have a servant's heart that is like Yours. Help me to not just do things or care for things, but to do them enthusiastically and with excellence, in a way that pleases You. I want to do it with all my might. Amen.

TODAY'S THOUGHT

God's people are people of excellence. They stand out from the crowd because they choose to do things well. They take care of what He's given to them and do it with excellence whether anybody is watching or not. Take the high road and make the more excellent choices.

Live Every Day with Excellence

Scripture Reading: Acts 9:36–43

In Joppa there was a disciple named Tabitha
(in Greek her name is Dorcas); she was always
doing good and helping the poor.

A c t s   9 : 3 6

Years ago, I was driving to the church building we occupied prior to our current home, and I noticed many in that area were not taking care of their homes or lawns. As I continued driving, I noticed one house that stood out in the midst of all those houses. The yard was immaculate. The house was painted. Everything was perfectly in place.

When I got to church, I commented on that house and somebody said, "Don't you know that's So-and-So's house? They're some of our most faithful members." That didn't surprise me one bit. Lakewood people are people of excellence.

As Dorcas did as reported in our scripture today, they stood out in the crowd. They were a cut above. They easily could have had the attitude, "Nobody else takes care of their homes. Why should we?" But they chose to have an excellent spirit.

You may be in a situation today in which everybody around you is being lazy, sloppy, and taking the easy way out. Don't let that rub off on you. You should be the one to have an excellent spirit. You should be the one to stand out in the crowd.

What kind of example is it to your friends, your neighbors, and your coworkers if your yard is sloppy and your car is never washed and you show up late to work? That's not a good representation, and the truth is that's not who you are. God made you as a person of excellence. Maybe all you've seen modeled is mediocrity or sloppiness—and maybe the people you work around are always late and undisciplined. But God is calling you to set a new standard.

He wants to take you places higher than you've ever dreamed of, but you've got to do your part and stir up the excellence on the inside. Don't make excuses. Don't say, "This is the way I've always been." Take this challenge and come up to a higher level of excellence.

TODAY'S PRAYER

Father, thank You that it doesn't matter what anybody else does or doesn't do, I can live my life with enthusiasm and stand out in a crowd as Dorcas did. I want to passionately fulfill my destiny, not just go through the motions. Fill me with Your joy so that other people will want what I have. Amen.

TODAY'S THOUGHT

Do you want your life to make an impact? You can change the atmosphere of your home or your entire office with a little bit of enthusiasm. Choose to be happy; live with excellence and integrity, and let the world know that you are enjoying the life God has given you!

Take Care of Yourself

Scripture Reading: 1 Corinthians 6

Do you not know that your bodies are temples of the Holy Spirit, who is in you, whom you have received from God? You are not your own; you were bought at a price. Therefore honor God with your bodies.

1 Corinthians 6:19–20

Excellence applies also to your personal appearance: the way you dress and the way you present yourself. We all have different styles and tastes. There is no right and wrong. The main thing is to present yourself in a way that you're proud of. Don't go out feeling less than your best or knowing that you didn't take the time to look like you should. You are the temple of the Most High God. He lives in you. Take time to take care of yourself.

Some women, in particular, take care of everyone else, putting their children first, being good wives, and running the house or doing their jobs. That's good, but they need to take care of themselves, too. Get your nails and hair done. Go shopping. Go exercise. Go have some fun with your friends. Take care of your temple in an excellent way.

Some men haven't bought new clothes in twenty-seven years. Their shirts have been in and out of style three times already. They're hard workers, taking care of their families. Now they need to take care of themselves, too.

One time I had just worked out when Victoria asked me to run to the grocery store. I was all sweaty, wearing an old, torn-up T-shirt and run-down gym shorts. My hair wasn't combed, but I didn't feel like getting cleaned up. So I just jumped in the car and headed to the store, hoping no one would notice me. I pulled into the parking lot and I heard God speak to me—not out loud, just an impression down inside—"Joel, don't you dare go in there like that. You are representing Me, the King of kings. I deserve respect and honor."

We have to understand that we represent almighty God. He does not like sloppiness. Even around the home, we all like to be super casual, but make sure you look good for your children and for your spouse.

Some ladies may need to get rid of bathrobes given to them by their great-grandmothers and buy something new. You may love them because they are comfortable and sentimental, but I'll tell you what nobody else will tell you: They are ugly. Go get something that makes you look like the masterpiece God made you to be.

TODAY'S PRAYER

Father, thank You for the privilege of being Your temple and for coming to dwell in my life. Help me to take care of my temple and adorn it in a way that brings honor and respect to You. Amen.

TODAY'S THOUGHT

Remember: You represent almighty God . . . all the time. How you live, how you dress, how you conduct your business and do your work, is all a reflection on our God. Aim for excellence in everything you do.

Make a Habit of Excellence

Scripture Reading: Luke 16

"Whoever can be trusted with very little can also be trusted with much, and whoever is dishonest with very little will also be dishonest with much."

Luke 16:10

When you go into a store and accidentally knock some clothes off the rack, don't pretend to not see them. A person of excellence picks them up and puts them back. When you're shopping for groceries and decide you shouldn't get the box of cookies, don't just stick it back over by the potato chips. A person of excellence takes the cookie box back where it was found. Well, you say, "That's what those employees are paid to do." You should do it unto God. You should do it because you have an excellent spirit.

A person of excellence doesn't park in the handicap spot because it's closer to the mall entrance or leave the lights on in their hotel room when leaving just because the hotel is paying for it. People of excellence go the extra mile to do what's right. They do that not because somebody is watching or making them. They do it to honor God. Sometimes you have to say, "God, I don't feel like doing this, but I will do it unto You."

At our house we used to get these very heavy, awkward five-gallon glass bottles of water, each with a neck, and you had to upend them and put them on a special dispenser to get the water out. Victoria likes everything super clean and insisted that the whole bottle get wiped down with soap, even the completely sealed receptor that goes way up inside the bottle's neck. There's no way you can even get to it except to break the seal. I debated with her several times, passionately stating that it wasn't necessary to wipe down the whole bottle, but I couldn't convince her, so I gave her my word that I would do it.

But there were many times I was in the pantry all by myself, and as I started to put the bottle up without cleaning it, I would hear that still small voice saying, "Joel, be a person of excellence. Keep your word." More than once, I had to take it down and get the soap.

Excellence is doing the right thing even when nobody can see you. Even when you don't think it's necessary. Even when you don't agree. Live up to your word.

TODAY'S PRAYER

Father, thank You that You gave me a conscience so I would have an inner rule by which to know right from wrong and be able to live as a person of excellence. When I start to compromise and hear that alarm go off, help me to listen. Help me to always do what I know in my heart is the right thing. Amen.

TODAY'S THOUGHT

God wants us to be people of integrity, people of honor, people who are trustworthy. A person of integrity is open and honest and true to his word. He doesn't need a legal contract to force him to fulfill his commitments. People of integrity are the same in private as they are in public. They do what's right whether anybody is watching or not.

Pass the Small Test

Scripture Reading: 1 Samuel 13

"Do not despise these small beginnings,
for the LORD rejoices to see the work begin . . ."
Zechariah 4:10 NLT

Many people do not enjoy God's favor like they should, because they don't pass the small tests. Being excellent may not be some huge adjustment you need to make. It may mean just leaving earlier so you get to work on time or not complaining when you have to clean up. It may mean not making personal phone calls on work time—just small things. But the Scripture says, "It's the little foxes that spoil the vines."

If I had put up that water bottle week after week without cleaning it, nobody would have known except God and me. I could have gotten away with it, but here's the key: I don't want something small to keep God from releasing something big into my life.

A while back, I was in a store's parking lot, and it was very windy outside. When I opened my car door, several pieces of trash blew out on the ground and flew about fifteen or twenty feet in different directions. I didn't feel like going over to pick up those scraps. I looked around and there were already all kinds of other trash in the parking lot.

I was in a hurry. I came up with several good excuses why I shouldn't go pick them up. I almost convinced myself to let them go, but at the last moment I decided I was going to be a person of excellence and pick up my trash. I ended up running all over that parking lot. My mind was saying, "What in the world am I doing out here? It doesn't matter—let the stuff go."

When I finally picked up all of the scattered trash, I came back to my car. I hadn't noticed a couple sitting in the car next to mine was watching the whole thing. They rolled the window down and said, "Hey, Joel. We watch you on television each week."

Then the lady said something very interesting. "We were watching to see what you were going to do."

I thought, "Oh, thank You, Jesus."

Whether you realize it or not, people are watching you. Make sure you're representing God the right way.

TODAY'S PRAYER

Father, thank You that You have said that we are the light of the world, and You have called us to let our light shine before others that they may see our good deeds and glorify You. I want to represent You in the right way, through my life, my house, my car, my clothes, my workplace, and my relationships. Help me have an excellent spirit in a way that I never have before. Amen.

TODAY'S THOUGHT

People are watching how you dress, how you care for your home, how you treat other people. They are trying to determine whether your words and your walk—your lifestyle— are consistent. What do they see? Are you compromising in so-called insignificant areas?

Distinguish Yourself

Scripture Reading: Daniel 2

Now Daniel so distinguished himself among the administrators and the satraps by his exceptional qualities that the king planned to set him over the whole kingdom.

Daniel 6:3

The Scripture says that Daniel had an excellent spirit. As a teenager, he was brought out of Judah into Babylon. The king had all these young men in training and the best of them would be chosen as the next leaders. They had a certain diet for them to eat and certain programs for them to follow. But Daniel had made a vow to God to always honor Him. Daniel was respectful, but he wouldn't eat the king's fancy foods. He didn't just go along with what everyone else was doing. He made the more excellent choice.

Scripture says, "Daniel so distinguished himself by his exceptional qualities that the king planned to put him over the whole kingdom." Notice it doesn't say: "God distinguished him and he got promoted." It says Daniel distinguished himself. *The Message* translation says, "Daniel completely outclassed the others." That's what happens when you honor God and have an excellent spirit. You don't compromise. You don't just go with the flow and do what everyone else is doing.

The Scripture goes on to say Daniel had incredible wisdom and understanding. He could interpret dreams and visions. When you have an excellent spirit, God will give you unprecedented favor, creativity, and ideas so that, like Daniel, you will stand out in the crowd. In humility, you will outclass those who don't honor God.

My question is: Are you distinguishing yourself and not waiting for God to do it? Are you doing more than you have to? Are you improving your skills? Examine your life. We all have areas in which we can strive for excellence, whether it's how we treat people, how we present ourselves, or how we develop our skills.

If you'll have a spirit of excellence, God will breathe in your direction and cause you to stand out. You'll look up and be more creative, more skilled, more talented, and wiser with more ideas. I believe and declare that like Daniel, you will outperform, outclass, and outshine, and God will promote you and set you in a place of honor. You can, you will.

TODAY'S PRAYER

Father, thank You that You didn't make me to just go with the flow and do what everyone else is doing. I commit myself to striving for excellence, whether it's in how I treat people, how I present myself to others, or how I develop my skills. I believe that as I honor You with my choices that You will breathe in my direction and cause me to stand out for Your glory. Amen.

TODAY'S THOUGHT

Don't let something small keep you from the big things God wants to do. You are called to be a cut above. You have excellence on the inside. It's who you are. Now do your part and be disciplined to bring out your excellence.

KEEP GROWING

Winners Never Stop Learning

Scripture Reading: Hebrews 5

And Jesus grew in wisdom and stature,
and in favor with God and man.
Luke 2:52

Too many people suffer from destination disease. They reach a certain level, earn their degrees, buy their dream homes, and then just coast.

Studies show that 50 percent of high school graduates never read another entire book. One reason may be that they see learning as something you do in school, just something you do for a period of life instead of as a way of life.

We all learned when we were in school. Our teachers, coaches, and parents taught us. We were expected to learn when we were school age. But some tend to think that once they finish a certain level of education: "I'm done with school. I've finished my training. I've got a good job."

Winners never stop learning, and this is the sixth undeniable quality I have observed. God did not create us to reach one level and then stop. Whether you're nine or ninety years old, you should constantly be learning, improving your skills, and getting better at what you do.

You have to take responsibility for your own growth. Growth is not automatic. What steps are you taking to improve? Are you reading books or listening to educational videos or audios? Are you taking any courses on the Internet or going to seminars? Do you have mentors? Are you gleaning information from people who know more than you?

Winners don't coast through life relying on what they have already learned. You have treasure on the inside—gifts, talents, and potential—put in you by the Creator of the universe. But those gifts will not automatically come out. They must be developed.

I read that the wealthiest places on earth are not the oil fields of the Middle East or the diamond mines of South Africa. The wealthiest places are the cemeteries. Buried in the ground are businesses that were never formed, books that were never written, songs that were never sung, dreams that never came to life, potential that was never released.

Don't go to your grave with that buried treasure. Keep growing. Keep learning. Every day we should have a goal to grow in some way, to learn something new.

TODAY'S PRAYER

Father, thank You for the treasure You put inside of me—
the talents and the potential—and all of the opportunities
You provide for my growth. I don't want to coast through life
relying on what I've already learned, but I want to do
everything I can to develop my gifts and potential. Amen.

TODAY'S THOUGHT

God has put more in you than you can even imagine. You
have gifts and talents that nobody else has. God is bringing
about new seasons of growth. Do not get stagnant and hold
on to the old. Keep growing, knowing that God has
something better in front of you.

Grow Your Gifts

Scripture Reading: Philippians 3

Not that I have already obtained all this, or have already arrived at my goal, but I press on to take hold of that for which Christ Jesus took hold of me.
Philippians 3:12

Pablo Casals was one of the greatest cellists of all time. He started playing at the age of twelve and accomplished things that no other cellist did. He was known around the world as the greatest in his field. Yet, at the age of eighty-five, Casals still practiced five hours a day. A reporter asked him why. He smiled and said, "I think I'm getting better."

Casals understood that when you stop learning, you stop growing. Whatever you do, get better at it. Sharpen your skills. Don't stay at the same level year after year.

There are all kinds of opportunities to increase. There is more knowledge available today than any time in history. You don't have to go to the library or to a university. With the Internet, information flows right into your home. The Internet wasn't created just to share pictures or play games. The Internet is a tool that can help you increase your gifts.

You have a responsibility not only to God, not only to your family, but also to yourself to develop what He's put in you. No matter what you do, you can always expand your knowledge and improve your skills. Read books to learn how to communicate, work as a team member, or lead more effectively. There are people who have gone where you're going. Listen to what they have to say. Turn off the TV and invest in yourself.

A lot of times we sit back and think, "God, I'm waiting on You. I'm waiting for that big break." That's the wrong attitude. Let me tell you who gets the big breaks—people who are prepared, those who develop their skills continuously. If you sharpen your skills, you won't need to work as hard. If you sharpen your skills, you'll get more done in less time. You will be more productive.

You should be doing something intentional and strategic every day to improve your skills. Don't be vague in your approach or say, "Well, Joel, I'm so busy. I don't have time to take any training courses. I don't have time to read books and learn new things. I'll get behind. When I have time, I'll do it." You are better than that. You've got too much in you to stay where you are. Your destiny is too great to get stuck.

TODAY'S PRAYER

Father, thank You for equipping me with everything I need to live an abundant life and to fulfill the destiny You have given me. Help me to do something intentional and strategic every day to improve my skills. I believe that as I do You will open doors for me that no man can shut. Amen.

TODAY'S THOUGHT

You've got to be proactive to take these steps to grow. When God sees you doing your part and developing what He's given you, He'll do His part and open up doors that no man can shut.

Don't Settle

Scripture Reading: 1 Samuel 16

So Samuel took the horn of oil and anointed him in the presence of his brothers, and from that day on the Spirit of the LORD came powerfully upon David.
1 Samuel 16:13

Whether you are a teacher, a carpenter, a banker, or a doctor, don't settle where you are. Don't coast or rest on your laurels. Stir up what God has put in you and get better at it.

Think about David in the Bible. He was out in the shepherd fields taking care of his father's sheep. In today's terms he had a boring minimum wage job and no friends, and it didn't look like there was any opportunity for growth. His brothers got the prestigious jobs in the army. David could have slacked off, been sloppy, and thought, "No reason to develop my skills. I have no opportunity. I'm stuck out here with these sheep."

Instead, while he was alone, he practiced using his slingshot day after day and month after month. I can envision him setting up a target, slinging rocks again and again, getting better, making adjustments, and sharpening his skills. He became a sharpshooter, a marksman, so precise, so skillful; he could hit a bull's-eye from a hundred meters away.

When God sought somebody to defeat a giant, somebody to lead His chosen people, He looked to see who was prepared. He wanted someone who had developed their skills, who had taken the time to cultivate the gifts He had put in them. He didn't choose just anybody—He selected a skilled marksman who could hit a target with precision.

In the same way, when God seeks somebody to promote, He doesn't just randomly close His eyes and say, "I'll pick this one. You won the lottery. It's your lucky day."

No, God looks for people who have developed their skills. When we read about David standing before Goliath and slinging that rock, sometimes we think it was all God's hand at work. In a sense it was God, but the truth is God didn't sling the rock. It was David who developed and used the skills God gave him.

Like David, God has put in you a set of special skills that will slay giant challenges and open new doors—skills that will thrust you to new levels. But here's the key: Your skills have to be developed. Every day you spend learning, growing, and improving will prepare you for that new level.

TODAY'S PRAYER

Father, thank You that You have put in me a set of special skills that will slay giant challenges and thrust me to new levels in my future. I believe that as I develop my skills and take advantage of opportunities to grow that You will open new doors for me. Amen.

TODAY'S THOUGHT

This is a call to action. There are new levels in your future. Things have shifted in your favor. God is looking for people who are prepared and taking steps to improve. He is looking for those who are serious about fulfilling their destinies.

Prepare Yourself to Be a Winner

Scripture Reading: Numbers 27:12–23

A man's gift makes room for him,
and brings him before great men.
PROVERBS 18:16 NKJV

You may be in a lower-position job, doing something that seems insignificant. But you know you have so much more in you. It would be easy to slack off and think, "There's no future here. I'll prepare as soon as I get out of this place, when good breaks come my way, or when the boss promotes me. Maybe then I'll take some courses, lose a few pounds, have a better attitude, and buy some nicer clothes."

That's backward. You must start improving right where you are. Start sharpening your skills while you're waiting. Study your manager's work habits. Study your best supervisor. Learn how to do their jobs. Be ready to step into those shoes.

When God sees you prepare yourself, He opens new doors. The Scripture says, "A man's gift makes room for him." If no new doors are opening, don't be discouraged. Just develop your gifts in a new way. Improve your skills.

You might feel that your supervisors aren't going anywhere right now, but if you outgrow them, outperform them, out produce them, and know more than them, your gifts will make room for you. Somewhere, somehow, and some way God will open a door and get you where He wants you to be.

Don't worry about who is ahead of you or when your time will come. Just keep growing, learning, and preparing. When you are ready, the right doors will open.

The fact is God may not want you to have your supervisor's position. That may be too low for you. He may want to thrust you right past your boss and put you at a whole new level. I know former receptionists who went from answering the phones to running multi-million-dollar companies.

You can. You will. Develop what's in you, and you'll go farther than you can imagine.

TODAY'S PRAYER

Father in Heaven, thank You that You have new levels
in front of me, new opportunities, new relationships,
promotions, and breakthroughs. You've been awesome in my life and I thank You for it. I believe that as
I keep stretching, keep growing, keep believing, and
keep dreaming that You will help me become everything You created me to be. Amen.

TODAY'S THOUGHT

In the coming days, God will bring opportunities
for you to increase your influence in amazing ways.
Don't shrink back in fear. Don't be intimidated. You are
well able. You are equipped. Dare to take those steps
of faith and sharpen your skills.

You Were Created to Increase

Scripture Reading: 2 Chronicles 22, especially vv. 13–14

Do you see someone skilled in their work? They will serve before kings; they will not serve before officials of low rank.
Proverbs 22:29

Have you come down with destination disease? You're comfortable with not learning anything new. Studies tell us that the average person only uses 11 percent of the brain. Think of all that potential you could be tapping into. Maybe you're an accountant. That's good, but why not get your CPA certification? That gift will make more room for you.

Maybe you're an electrician, a plumber, or a mechanic. That's great, but what steps are you taking to improve your skills and your position in life? If you spend two hours a day improving on the same skills, in three years you will be an expert in that area. In today's competitive marketplace, with the economy so tight and business so bottom-line oriented, if you're not improving then you're falling behind. If your skill levels are at the same place today they were five years ago, you're at a disadvantage.

I want to light a new fire under you. Shake off that destination disease. Sharpen your skills. I read an article about reducing the risk of being laid off. There were three main things that employers look for in determining who stays. They look for those with positive attitudes, flexibility, and the desire to keep learning and improving.

To be a winner, you need to develop your gifts to the point where your company can't make it without you. Or at least, you want your bosses to know things don't run nearly as smoothly when you're gone. If you're out for a week and nobody misses you, that's okay as long as you own the company, but if you're an employee, that's alarming. If you're not being missed, maybe you're not needed.

You need to kick it into a new gear. Produce more than you've been producing. Take some classes to increase your skills. Step it up a notch. Don't settle for a low position where no one will miss you. You have treasure in you. There is talent and skill that will cause you to be noticed. Keep sharpening your skills. Cream always rises to the top.

TODAY'S PRAYER

Father, thank You that You are taking me to a land of abundance, a place like I've never experienced before. I want to kick it into a new gear and prepare myself and develop those skills so that I can fulfill my destiny. I believe that You will fill me with wisdom and use my gifts and strengths to bring great glory to Your name. Amen.

TODAY'S THOUGHT

Don't make the mistake of settling for "good enough." Good enough is not your destiny. When you have an excellent spirit, it shows up in the quality of your work and the attitude with which you do it. You are a child of the Most High God, and you were created to excel. Keep reaching forward to the new things God has in store.

Be the Solution, Not the Problem

Scripture Reading: Genesis 41

The LORD was with Joseph so that he prospered,
and he lived in the house of his Egyptian master.
When his master saw that the LORD was with him and that
the LORD gave him success in everything he did, . . .
Potiphar . . . entrusted to his care everything he owned.

Genesis 39:2–4

Remember the story of Joseph in the Bible? He started off at the very bottom. He was thrown into a pit and sold into slavery by his brothers. Joseph didn't wait for vindication. He decided to be his best. Even as a slave, he developed his gifts. He made himself so valuable that he was put in charge of his master's house. When he was falsely accused and put in prison, he was so wise and skillful that they put him in charge of the prison.

Joseph was cream rising to the top. When Pharaoh needed someone to run the country and administer the nationwide food program, he didn't choose one of his own department heads or a cabinet member. He chose Joseph, a prisoner and a foreigner. Why? Joseph developed his skills right where he was, and his gifts made room for him.

Don't use where you are as an excuse to not grow. Don't say, "I'm not in a good job. I don't like my position. I've had unfair things happen." Remember, the treasure is still in you. It's time to use your gifts. Stretch yourself. You should be so productive, so filled with wisdom that no matter where you are, like Joseph, you will rise to the top.

One way you'll be invaluable is to learn to be a problem solver. That's what Joseph was. He was solution oriented. Don't go to your boss and say, "Our department is falling apart. This manager is about to quit. What do you want me to do?" That's not the way to get promoted. If you present a problem, always present a solution as well. If you can't present a solution, hold it until you can figure out something.

A child can come tell me the building is on fire. That's easy. That doesn't take any skill. But I want somebody to tell me that not only is the building on fire, but also the fire department is on the way, all the people are safe, the insurance company has been notified, and temporary quarters have been arranged. If you want to be invaluable to your organization, present your bosses with solutions, not problems.

TODAY'S PRAYER

Father, today I declare that my hope and my trust are in You. Even when I don't understand my circumstances, I know You are working things out for my good. Help me to bloom where I'm planted and be a problem solver at all times. Amen.

TODAY'S THOUGHT

If you want to see change, if you want to see God open new doors, the key is to bloom right where you are planted by solving problems every day. You cannot wait until everything becomes better before you decide to have a good attitude. You have to be the best you can be right where you are.

Have a Personal Growth Plan

Scripture Reading: 2 Timothy 2

*Do your best to present yourself to God as
one approved, a worker who does not need to be ashamed
and who correctly handles the word of truth.*
2 Timothy 2:15

What steps are you taking to better yourself so you can go to the next level? Are you reading books and trade magazines to stay up-to-date? Can you take a course to gain an advantage? You've got to be on the offensive, even if you have your degree. Do you know that many degrees are outdated in as little as five years? The world is changing so fast. If you don't continue learning and keep growing, you will fall behind. Will Rogers said, "Even if you're on the right track, if you just sit there, eventually you're going to get run over."

God has new levels in your future, but if you're not prepared for them, you can miss out on the fullness of what He has in store. Every one of us should have a personal growth plan. Not something vague: "I'll read a book every once in a while. I'll take the company training this year." No, you need a specific plan that lays out how you're going to grow. It should include the steps you will take to get better.

Let me give you some ideas. The average American spends three hundred hours a year in a car. Imagine what you can learn in three hundred hours. Take advantage of the valuable time by turning your car into a university. Instead of listening to the radio driving to work, listen to good teaching audiobooks and CDs, training materials, and other helpful material that will help you grow and improve in your field.

You can also listen to inspiring and informative audios while working out or before you go to bed. Podcasts are another great tool. You can download messages and listen to them whenever you want. This year we will give away 100 million copies of my messages at no charge. You can sign up for them on iTunes and listen as often as you want. That's a growth plan.

These are simple things winners do to keep growing and bettering themselves. You don't have to spend three hours a day studying. Just take advantage of the time you're not using right now.

TODAY'S PRAYER

Father, I know that You have so much more in store for me and that You want me to stretch and better myself. Help me to break out of my coasting rut and give me wisdom to take advantage of my time and energies to pursue the things that You have placed in my heart. Amen.

TODAY'S THOUGHT

Don't fall into a complacency trap. Where you are may not be a bad place, but you know it's not where you're supposed to be. You're not developing the treasure God has put in you. Pursue the excellence that God has placed in your heart.

Associate with the Right People

Scripture Reading: Exodus 18

Whatever you have learned or received or
heard from me, or seen in me—put it into practice.
And the God of peace will be with you.
Philippians 4:9

If you want to keep growing, you need to have good mentors, people who have been where you want to go, people who know more than you. Let them speak into your life. Listen to their ideas. Learn from their mistakes. Study how they think and how they got to where they are.

I heard about a company that held a sales class for several hundred employees. The speaker asked if anyone knew the names of the top three salespeople. Every person raised a hand. He then asked how many of them had gone to lunch with these top salespeople and taken time to find out how they do what they do. Not one hand went up.

There are people all around us whom God put in our paths on purpose so we can gain wisdom, insight, and experience, but we have to be open to learning from them. Look around and find the winners from whom you can learn.

I say this respectfully: Don't waste your valuable time with people who aren't contributing to your growth. Life is too short to hang around people who are not going anywhere. Destination disease is contagious. If you're with them long enough, their lack of ambition and energy will rub off on you.

Winners need to associate with inspiring people who build you up, people who challenge you to go higher, not anyone who pulls you down and convinces you to settle where you are. Your destiny is too important for that.

TODAY'S PRAYER

Father, thank You that You have placed people around me from whom I can gain wisdom, insight, and experience. Help me to be brave enough to stop spending time with people who aren't going anywhere, and help me to rather put my time into people who will contribute to my growth and challenge me to go higher. Amen.

TODAY'S THOUGHT

It's time for you to soar with the eagles rather than be pecking around with the chickens. Spend time with people who inspire you to reach for new heights. If you associate with successful people, before long their enthusiasm will be contagious and you will catch that vision.

Build a Foundation for Growth

Scripture Reading: Acts 18

*Do not be so deceived and misled! Evil companionships
(communion, associations) corrupt and deprave
good manners and morals and character.*

1 Corinthians 15:33 AMP

Young people often get caught up in trying to be popular instead of trying to be their best. I've found that in twenty years nobody will care whether you were popular in high school. Those who need attention and act up or wear a lot of bling and don't study because it isn't cool will find things change after high school. What matters, then, is having a good education, good work habits, and a good attitude that gives you a foundation to build on.

In most schools, the science fair is not the most popular event. Being in the math club isn't nearly as cool as being on the football team. Some of my friends made fun of people on the debate team, but now they work for people who were on the debate team.

Junior high and high school are critical times in our lives and our formative years. There's so much emphasis on sports. I love sports and played sports growing up, and I still do. They teach discipline and teamwork and perseverance, and that's all great. But we need to keep sports in perspective. Most of us are not going to play sports for a living. One in one million kids will play professional basketball. The average professional football career is three and a half years. Even if you do make it, you still need a good foundation for life after football.

When you study and learn and take school seriously, you may be called a bookworm, a geek, or a nerd, but don't worry about those names. In a few years you'll be called the boss. You'll be called CEO, president, senator, pastor, or doctor.

Thomas Edison, Henry Ford, and Harvey Firestone had summer homes next to one another in Florida. They were close friends and spent much of their summers together.

Who you associate with makes a difference in how far you go in life. If your friends are Larry, Curly, and Moe, you may have fun, but you may not be going anywhere.

TODAY'S PRAYER

Father, thank You that created me to do great things, and You've put talent, ability, and skills on the inside that are waiting to be developed. I don't want to be restricted by my environment and associating with the wrong people. Help me to redeem the time and give me the wisdom to surround myself with inspiring people who build me up and challenge me to rise higher. Amen.

TODAY'S THOUGHT

Beware of associating with or adopting the attitudes of people who, through their negative outlook and lack of self-esteem, will rob you of the greatness that God has for you. It is amazing what can happen when you get into an atmosphere where people build you up rather than tear you down, where people encourage and challenge you to be the best you can be.

Be Strategic and Intentional

Scripture Reading: 1 Samuel 23

And Saul's son Jonathan went to David
at Horesh and helped him find strength in God.
1 Samuel 23:16

You're not being responsible with what God gave you if you're hanging out with time wasters who have no goals and no dreams. You have a destiny to fulfill. God has amazing things in your future. It's critical that you surround yourself with the right people. If you're the smartest one in your group, then your group is too small. You need to be around people who know more than you; winners who are farther along than you and can inspire you and challenge you to rise higher. Don't be intimidated by them; be inspired.

If you take an oak tree seed and plant it in a five-gallon pot, that tree will never grow to the size it was created to be. Why? It's restricted by the size of the pot. In the same way, God has created you to do great things. He's put talent, ability, and skills on the inside. You don't want to be restricted by your environment. The people you hang around with may think small or be negative and drag you down. You need to get out of that little pot because God created you to soar. It's fine to help people in need, but don't spend all your time with them.

My question for you is this: Are you doing anything strategic and intentional to keep growing? If not, start right now. Come up with a personal growth plan. It can be something like, "I will get up every morning and spend the first twenty minutes meditating on the Scripture. I will listen to a teaching CD driving to work. I will read a book fifteen minutes every night before I go to bed. I will meet with my mentor twice a month. I will be in church every weekend." That's a definite plan. When you take responsibility for your growth, God will honor your efforts.

Promotion, good breaks, businesses, books, and divine connections are in your future. There is treasure in you, waiting to be developed. Redeem the time. Make a decision to grow in some way every day. God promises your gifts will make room for you.

Because you are prepared, I believe and declare God is about to thrust you into the fullness of your destiny. He will open doors that no man can shut. You will go further than you could imagine and become the winner He's created you to be.

TODAY'S PRAYER

Father, thank You that You created me to soar and
to do great things. You've given me talent, ability, and skills.
I believe that as I prepare and take responsibility with
my growth, You will honor my efforts and take me
further than I can ever imagine. Amen.

TODAY'S THOUGHT

Have you surrounded yourself with the right people?
From whom are you learning wisdom, insight, and
experience? How can you expand your circle of those
who inspire you to go to higher levels?

SERVE
OTHERS

You Were Created to Serve

Scripture Reading: Matthew 20

"Whoever wants to become great among you must be your servant, and whoever wants to be first must be your slave— just as the Son of Man did not come to be served, but to serve, and to give his life as a ransom for many."
Matthew 20:26–28

Jesus said, "If you want to be great in the kingdom, if you want to live a blessed life, there's a simple key: You have to serve other people." He wasn't talking about an event that happens every once in a while. He was talking about a lifestyle in which you live to help others, and you're always looking for ways to serve.

When you live a "serve others" lifestyle, you help friends, volunteer in your community, and take care of loved ones. It's not something you have to force yourself to do. It becomes a part of who you are. You develop an attitude of giving to everyone you meet. You'll have true happiness and fulfillment when you live to give, not to receive.

Many people are not happy, because they are focused only on themselves. It's all about "my dreams, my goals, and my problems." That self-centered focus will limit you. You were created to give. God has put people in your life on purpose so you can be a blessing to them. Every morning you should ask, ' God, what is my assignment today? Help me to see the people you want me to be good to."

I've known my friend Johnny my whole life, more than forty years. He is constantly serving others. He's always running somebody to the airport, taking a friend to dinner, or helping somebody on a project. When my father was on dialysis, if one of the family members couldn't take him to the clinic, we'd ask Johnny and he'd gladly do it.

I called Johnny one hot Saturday afternoon. When he answered the phone, it was very noisy in the background. I asked him where he was. He said, "I'm on top of a house. My friend's next door neighbor is an elderly lady, and we told her we'd re-roof her house this weekend." He didn't even know the lady. She was just the neighbor of a friend. But Johnny has developed this mentality to serve others.

When you serve others, you are serving God.

TODAY'S PRAYER

Father, thank You that You created me to serve others,
to be blessed by giving to others, to be truly fulfilled by
making the lives of others better. God, what is my assignment
today? Help me to see the people You want me to be good to,
the ones who need what I have, and the ones who
need my love and encouragement. Amen.

TODAY'S THOUGHT

Friend, the closest thing to the heart of our God is helping
hurting people. God loves when we sing and worship and
pray. But nothing pleases God more than when we care for
His children. Be on the lookout for somebody you can bless.

Your Reward Is Coming

Scripture Reading: Matthew 10

*"And if anyone gives even a cup of cold water to
one of these little ones who is my disciple, truly I tell you,
that person will certainly not lose their reward."*
Matthew 10:42

Jesus said, "If you give a cup of cold water to someone in need, you will surely be rewarded." Every time you serve, God sees it. Every time you help someone else. Every time you sacrifice—you go out of your way to pick up a friend, you get up early to sing in the choir, you stay late to help a coworker— God is keeping the record.

Don't look for people to pay you back. They may not thank you. You may not get the credit. There may be no applause, but let me assure you that when you serve others, there is applause in heaven. God sees your sacrifices.

J.J. Moses was a star football player in college. He was drafted by the Houston Texans and played for them for six years. As the kick returner and punt returner, he was amazing to watch, as fast as lightning, darting here and there! Playing in the National Football League in front of millions of fans, J.J. was at the pinnacle of success.

But during the off seasons—and any time he didn't have a game—do you know where J.J. was every Saturday night? J.J. was not at home with his feet up or out enjoying his celebrity. He was at our church in Houston, serving others as an usher, helping people to their seats, passing the offering plates, and making everyone feel welcome.

Many of those who came to church didn't know he was a star football player. In the stadium all the lights were on him. Fans wanted his autograph or pictures with him. J.J. could have allowed his fame to go to his head and thought, "I'm big-time. I'm not serving as an usher. They can wait on me." Instead, J.J. told me, "My greatest honor was not playing in front of eighty thousand people in the stadium each week. My greatest honor was ushering in my section at Lakewood every Saturday night."

You don't need people's applause. You don't need anyone cheering you on. You don't need the Employee of the Month plaque; you are doing it unto God. He's the One who matters. When you serve others—volunteering at the hospital or in the church nursery, taking your neighbor to the doctor—God says you'll be great in the kingdom.

TODAY'S PRAYER

Father, thank You that every time I serve someone, You see it. I don't need the applause of others, but I'm thrilled to know that as I give, You keep a record of it. I would love to be great in and for Your kingdom! Amen.

TODAY'S THOUGHT

Giving is a spiritual principle. Whatever you give will be given back to you. If you are generous to people in their time of need, God will make sure that other people are generous to you in your time of need. What you make happen for others, God will make happen for you.

Make the Lives of Others Better

Scripture Reading: John 3

For God so loved the world,
that he gave his only begotten Son.
John 3:16 KJV

If you want a great life, it doesn't just come from success, having a bigger house, or more accomplishments. There's nothing wrong with those things. God wants you to be blessed. But if you want to truly be fulfilled, you have to develop the habit of serving others.

I knew a man whose wealth was estimated at more than nine billion dollars. He's in heaven now, but he'd made it big in the oil business after starting with nothing. He loved God and always helped others. Among many other things, he owned a big retreat center where people could come and get away for a weekend and be refreshed.

One time a couple showed up at the retreat's front desk when the receptionist had stepped away. My friend the multibillionaire just happened to be there. He was an older man, very friendly and humble. He checked in the couple, gave them their keys, then grabbed their suitcases and carried them to the room. He set them up, laid out their bags, and even brought ice for them.

He was about to leave them when the lady pulled a five-dollar bill from her purse and gave him a tip. She thought he was the bellman.

He just smiled and said, "Thank you, Lord. Now I've got nine billion and five dollars!"

I love the fact that he wasn't too important to serve. He didn't say, "Excuse me, I don't need a tip. I own it all. Do you know who I am?"

You are never too big, never too important, and never too influential to serve. It takes a big person to do something small. It takes humility to say, "I don't have to do this. It's not required of me. I could have somebody else do it. Nobody would fault me if I didn't, but I know in order to serve God, I need to serve other people."

You were created to give. You were created to make the lives of others better. Someone needs what you have. Someone needs your love. Someone needs your smile. Someone needs your encouragement and your gifts.

TODAY'S PRAYER

Father, thank You that You were willing to give Your only begotten Son for us. I want to be a giver like You are and not a taker. I believe that as I learn the simple secret of serving others and living to give that You will bring me into my full potential as a person. Amen.

TODAY'S THOUGHT

We were not made to function as self-involved people, thinking only of ourselves. No, God created us to be givers. And you will never be truly fulfilled as a human being until you learn the simple secret of how to give your life away. Have an attitude that says, "Who can I serve today?"

Feed Your Soul Through Serving

Scripture Reading: John 4

"My food," said Jesus, "is to do the will of him
who sent me and to finish his work."
John 4:34

When you serve others, there will be a satisfaction that money can't buy. You'll feel a peace, a joy, a strength, and a fulfillment that only God can give. The Bible tells a story about Jesus and the disciples traveling a long way to Samaria. They were tired and hungry. Jesus sent the disciples into town to get food while He waited at the well. There He met a woman. He told her about her future and gave her a new beginning.

The disciples came back a few hours later with the food, but Jesus wasn't hungry anymore. He wasn't tired, either. He was sitting by the well satisfied, at peace. They were surprised. They tried to offer Him something to eat, but He wouldn't take it. He said, "I have food that you know nothing about." They thought maybe somebody came while they were gone and gave Him something to eat. They talked about it: "He was tired, but now He's refreshed. He was hungry, but now He says He's satisfied. How could that be?"

Jesus overheard them trying to figure it out. He told them the secret. He said, "My meat is to do the will of Him that sent me, to accomplish His work." He was saying, "I get fed by doing what God wants me to do. I get nourished when I help people. My food, strength, peace, joy, and satisfaction come when I serve others."

When you do the will of your Father, it doesn't drain you; it replenishes you. You feel energized, stronger, and refreshed. You may volunteer in your community each week. You may get up early and go to church on your day off, maybe serving in the children's ministry after working all week. You may clean houses in the community outreach Saturday morning. You may spend the afternoon at the prison encouraging the inmates. You'd think you would leave tired, worn out, run-down, and needing to go home and rest after volunteering all day. But just like with Jesus, when you help others, you get fed.

Strength, joy, energy, peace, wisdom, and healing come to those who serve. You should be run-down, but God reenergizes and refreshes you so that at the end of the day you aren't down, you are up. You don't leave low, you leave high. God pays you back.

TODAY'S PRAYER

Father, thank You that Your Son Jesus, who had all
of the power and authority in the world, modeled a servant
attitude that overflowed with joy. Thank You for the strength,
joy, energy, peace, wisdom, and healing that come when
I humble myself and serve others. Amen.

TODAY'S THOUGHT

When you center your life around yourself, not only do you
miss out on God's best, but you rob other people of the joy
and blessings that God wants to give them through you.
Quit trying to figure out what everybody can do for you,
get your mind off yourself, start trying to figure out
what you can do for somebody else, and go do it.

DAY 5

Lift Others and God Will Lift You

Scripture Reading: Acts 3

One person gives freely, yet gains even more; another withholds unduly, but comes to poverty. A generous person will prosper; whoever refreshes others will be refreshed.
Proverbs 11:24–25

Every time I leave one of our church services, I feel stronger than when I came in. It doesn't make natural sense. I put out a lot of energy, spend long hours, and shake a lot of hands, but I go home reenergized. Why? Because when you serve others, making their lives better, lifting them, healing those who are hurting, you are blessing them and being blessed yourself. You are being fed. You're being filled back up.

If you're always tired and run-down, it may be that you're not doing enough for others. You've got to get your mind off yourself. Go to a retirement home and cheer up someone who is lonely. Bake your neighbor a cake. Coach the Little League team.

As you lift others, God will lift you. This should not be something you do every once in a while, when you have extra time. This should be a lifestyle, where it's a part of your nature. You don't have to do something big—small acts of kindness are just fine. A simple word of encouragement can make someone's day.

Victoria was walking through the crowded church hallway after a service one day when she saw a young lady coming toward her. As she passed her, Victoria looked her in the eyes

169

and said, "You are so beautiful." They had a five-second conversation and then went on their ways. That young lady told me a couple of weeks later that Victoria's small kindness marked a turning point in her life. She had been through an abusive relationship. She felt so unattractive, so bad about herself, and beaten down by life.

She said when Victoria told her that she was beautiful, it was as if she'd broken the chains holding her back. Something came back to life inside her. The Scripture says, "A kind word works wonders." All through the day we can serve God by speaking kind words, offering compliments, giving encouragement, and lifting up those around us.

"You look great today." "I appreciate you." "I believe in you." "I'm praying for your family."

TODAY'S PRAYER

Father, thank You that I don't have to be extraordinary
to lift others up. All through the day help me to speak kind
words, offer compliments, give encouragement, and lift up
those around me. I believe that as I lift others,
You will lift me. Amen.

TODAY'S THOUGHT

Perhaps you feel you have nothing to give. Sure you do! You can give a smile or a hug. You can do some menial but meaningful task to help someone. You can visit someone in the hospital or make a meal for a person who is shut in. You can write an encouraging letter. Somebody needs your friendship.

Be Like Jesus

Scripture Reading: Philippians 2

You must have the same attitude that Christ Jesus had. Though he was God, he did not think of equality with God as something to cling to. Instead, he gave up his divine privileges; he took the humble position of a slave and was born as a human being. When he appeared in human form, he humbled himself in obedience to God and died a criminal's death on a cross.

Philippians 2:5–8 NLT

It's great to serve other people, but don't forget to serve your own family. Husbands should serve their wives. "Honey, I'm going in the kitchen. Can I bring you anything?" "Let me run and fill up your car's gas tank so you won't have to do it tomorrow."

If we all had this servant's attitude toward our spouses, more marriages could stay together. I know men who expect their wives to do everything for them—cook, clean, wash the clothes, keep the house straightened up. That's not a wife; that's a maid! If you want a wife—a friend, a lover, and someone to make your life great—you have to be willing to serve her. Bring her breakfast in bed. Pick up your own dirty clothes. Help with the children. Make her feel special. Marriage is not a dictatorship. It's a partnership!

You might say: "Well, Joel, the Bible says the wife should submit to the husband." Yes, but it also says the husband should love his wife like Christ loved the church.

Jesus Christ modeled a servant attitude that overflowed with joy. He had all the power in the world. He was the most influential man who ever lived. Yet He bowed down and washed His disciples' feet. He could have asked any of the disciples and they would have done it. He could have called an angel and said, "Hey, do me a favor. Wash their feet. They stink. Peter needs some Odor Eaters! I don't want to deal with it today."

Instead, Jesus pulled out His towel, bowed down, and washed their feet one by one. He gave us His example of service to others so we would know we're never too important or successful to bow down low and serve another person. The more you walk in humility, and the more willing you are to serve others, the higher God can take you.

If you are married, try serving your spouse more, and you'll see your marriage rise to a new level of happiness.

TODAY'S PRAYER

Father, thank You that You always took time with people.
You were always willing to stop and help a person in need.
I humble myself before You and especially ask You to help me
serve my loved ones with overflowing joy. Amen.

TODAY'S THOUGHT

Jesus was never too busy with His own agenda,
with His own plans. He wasn't so caught up in Himself that
He was unwilling to stop and help a person in need. Jesus
freely gave of His life. I believe He demands nothing less
from those who claim to be His followers today.

Look for Others to Bless

Scripture Reading: Matthew 25

"Or when did we see You sick, or in prison, and come to You?"
And the King will answer and say to them, "Assuredly,
I say to you, inasmuch as you did it to one of the least
of these My brethren, you did it to Me."

Matthew 25:39–40 NKJV

In a Saturday service a while ago, I was baptizing people, and among them was an older man who'd had a stroke. He was in a wheelchair and couldn't walk. The younger man pushing him in the wheelchair was about my age. You could tell that he really cared about the man. He went to great lengths to make sure he was okay.

To get in the church baptistery, you have to go up some stairs and then walk down stairs into the water. A couple of men helped the older man stand up. Then the younger man put his arms under his legs and his back so he could carry the elderly man into the water, just like you'd carry a sleeping baby. It was a very moving scene, watching the younger man help someone so determined to be baptized despite his age and disabilities.

With the young man's help, we were able to baptize the elderly man. After we returned him to his wheelchair, I asked the younger man: "Is that your father?" He shook his head no. "Is he your uncle or your relative?" I asked.

The younger man explained that they'd just met in church a few weeks earlier. On the Sunday I announced the baptism date, the older man in the wheelchair turned to him and said, "I wish I could be baptized, but I had this stroke." The young man offered to help him. The elderly man said he didn't have any family to bring him to church. The young man said, "Don't worry. I'll take care of you." And he did, even though they'd only met once before in church. I love the fact this young man was just quietly serving this man.

I will never forget the image of that young man carrying the crippled man into the water. Helping less fortunate people is the closest thing to the heart of God. Jesus said, "When you do it to the least of these, you're doing it unto Me." Remember that when you go out of your way to be good to others or when you make sacrifices no one knows about, God sees what you are doing. He sees your heart of compassion. Maybe no one else on this earth is singing your praises, but up there all of heaven is cheering you on.

TODAY'S PRAYER

Father God, help me to have the same heart of compassion as the young man who helped the man with the stroke. Help me not to be so busy, so caught up in my own life that I miss opportunities to serve others. I want to do the things that are on Your heart for others. Amen.

TODAY'S THOUGHT

God asks us to carry others in need. Maybe you won't have to carry them physically, but instead just lighten their loads. Will you help bring their dreams to pass? Will you go out of your way to be good to them?

Cheers in Heaven

Scripture Reading: Acts 7

*"Watch out! Don't do your good deeds publicly, to be admired
by others, for you will lose the reward from your Father in
heaven. . . . But when you give to someone in need, don't let your
left hand know what your right hand is doing. Give your gifts in
private, and your Father, who sees everything, will reward you."*

Matthew 6:1–4 NLT

As a leader of Lakewood Church, I receive rewards for my work from those who thank me, clap for me, and cheer me on. I'm very grateful. But when no one is clapping for you, when you're not being thanked, or no recognition comes your way, don't become discouraged and think you're being overlooked. Your reward will be greater.

If people give you credit, you have received a portion of your reward. When nobody gives you credit, the Scripture says, "What you do in secret, God will reward you for in the open." When it comes time for the rewards to be passed out, some of us in the front will have to step back. Then there will be greater rewards handed out to those who worked behind the scenes without recognition, giving their time, money, and energy.

Not long ago one of our ushers went to be with the Lord. He had volunteered faithfully at Lakewood Church for nearly thirty years. You could count on him to be helping people every week with a pleasant smile and always dressed well. One of his requests was that he would be buried wearing his Lakewood usher's badge. So, at his funeral, the badge he'd worn for thirty years was pinned to his favorite suit. He could have been buried with a lot of other things, but he was so honored to serve others.

When our former usher entered heaven, I believe there was a great celebration. I can imagine angels singing, trumpets blowing, people clapping, and an amazing welcoming-home ceremony. There wasn't a lot of applause and fanfare down here for his life of service and kindness, but it did not go unnoticed. It will be rewarded.

The Scripture says when Stephen went to heaven, Jesus stood up to welcome him. Jesus is normally seated at the right hand of the Father, but I believe there are times when Jesus says, "You know what? This one deserves a standing ovation."

TODAY'S PRAYER

Father, thank You for the many opportunities You give me to serve others. Your Son came not to be served, but to serve and to give His life as a ransom for me, and I want to reflect His servant's heart in all that I do. Amen.

TODAY'S THOUGHT

Friend, don't let anybody convince you that it doesn't make any difference how you live. God sees your acts of kindness and loving service to meet others' needs. He's observed every time you went out of the way to lend a helping hand. It pleases God when you serve others, and the day is coming when He will pour out His rewards upon you.

You're Not Home Yet

Scripture Reading: Hebrews 6

God is not unjust; he will not forget your work
and the love you have shown him as you have helped
his people and continue to help them.

Hebrews 6:10

I heard about an older missionary couple who served more than sixty years in Africa helping less fortunate people and did so much good. When they finally retired and returned home to New York, they were booked on the same ship as President Teddy Roosevelt, who was returning from a big hunting expedition. When their ship pulled into the dock, a band was playing, and the mayor and other dignitaries were lined up. Flags waved. Confetti rained down from buildings. It was a huge celebration. When the president walked off the ship, the huge crowd cheered, waved, and took photos.

The missionary watched all this and said to his wife, "It doesn't seem right that we've given our lives to serve, to give, and to make a difference, and the president just goes on a big vacation and the whole world welcomes him home. Nobody even knows we exist."

The missionary felt very discouraged as they walked off the boat. Later that night, he prayed, "God, I don't understand. We return and nobody even knows we're here." He heard God's reply come from within his heart: "Son, it's because you're not home yet."

You will be rewarded. There will be a celebration like you've never seen. The angels will be singing, and all of heaven will join in to welcome you home. If you have been faithful, sacrificed, volunteered, and given to others, be encouraged today. God sees every act of kindness. He sees every good deed. Nothing you've done has gone unnoticed. God saw it, and the good news is you will be rewarded.

Remember, when you do what God asks, you will be fed, refreshed, strengthened, and reenergized. Be on the lookout for ways you can be good to people. If you develop a lifestyle of serving others, God promises you will be great in the kingdom. I believe and declare because you're a giver, you will come in to your reward. You will come in to health, strength, opportunity, promotion, and breakthroughs. You will come into new levels of God's goodness.

TODAY'S PRAYER

Father God, thank You that You see every act of kindness and every good deed. I believe that as I do for others what You ask of me, I am doing it for You as well, and I am delighted that the day will come when You reward me for it. I look forward to the celebration with all of heaven joining in. Amen.

TODAY'S THOUGHT

God sees your heart. Nothing you do goes unnoticed by God. He's keeping the records, and He will reward you in due time. When you bless someone else, you never lose out. Even if someone takes advantage of your good nature, God will not allow your generosity to go unrewarded.

SECTION VIII

Stay
PASSIONATE

Get Your Passion Back

Scripture Reading: Galatians 6

Let us not be weary in well doing:
for in due season we shall reap, if we faint not.
Galatians 6:9 KJV

Studies show that enthusiastic people get better breaks. They're promoted more often, have higher incomes, and live happier lives. That's not a coincidence. The word *enthusiasm* comes from the Greek word *entheos*. *Theos* is a term for "God." When you're enthusiastic, you are full of God. You get up in the morning excited about life, recognizing that each day is a gift. You are motivated to pursue your goals and succeed.

The eighth undeniable quality of a winner is that they stay passionate throughout their lives. Too many people have lost their enthusiasm. At one time they were excited about their futures and passionate about their dreams, but along the way they hit some setbacks. They didn't get the promotions they wanted, maybe a relationship didn't work out, or they had health issues. Something took the wind out of their sails. They're just going through the motions of life; getting up, going to work, and coming home.

On January 15, 2009, Capt. Chesley "Sully" Sullenberger successfully landed a disabled jet airplane in the icy Hudson River and all 155 passengers and crew members survived. It's known as the "Miracle on the Hudson." Just after the successful rescue, a reporter asked a cold and wet passenger what he thought about surviving that frightening event. The passenger had a glow on his face and excitement in his voice when he replied: "I was alive before, but now I'm *really* alive." He recognized each moment as a gift and decided that instead of just living, he would start really living.

God didn't breathe His life into us so we would drag through the day. He didn't create us in His image, crown us with His favor, and equip us with His power so that we would have no enthusiasm. You may have had some setbacks, but this is a new day. God is breathing new life into you. If you shake off the blahs and get your passion back, the winds will start blowing once again—not against you, but for you. When you get in agreement with God, He will cause things to shift in your favor.

TODAY'S PRAYER

Father God, You didn't breathe Your life into me so I would drag through the day. You didn't create me in Your image, crown me with Your favor, and equip me with Your power so that I would have no enthusiasm. I'm shaking off the blahs and getting my passion back, and I believe You are causing things to shift in my favor. Amen.

TODAY'S THOUGHT

One of the main reasons we lose our enthusiasm in life is because we start to take for granted what God has done for us. Don't allow your relationship with Him to become stale or your appreciation for His goodness to become common. Don't take for granted the greatest gift of all that God has given you—Himself!

Seeds of Greatness

Scripture Reading: 2 Timothy 1

*For this reason I remind you to fan into flame the gift of God,
which is in you through the laying on of my hands.*
2 Timothy 1:6

Are you really alive? Are you passionate about your life or are you stuck in a rut, letting the pressures of life weigh you down or taking for granted what you have? You weren't created to simply exist or to go through the motions; you were created to be really alive.

You have seeds of greatness on the inside. There's something more for you to accomplish. The day you quit being excited about your future is the day you quit living. When you quit being passionate about your future, you go from living to merely existing.

In the natural there may not be anything for you to be excited about. When you look into the future, all you see is more of the same. You have to be strong and say, "I refuse to drag through this day with no passion. I am grateful that I'm alive and that I have opportunities before me. I'm not just alive—I'm really alive."

This is what Paul told Timothy in the Bible: "Stir up the gift, fan the flame." When you stir up the passion, your faith will allow God to do amazing things. If you want to remain passionate, you cannot let what once was a miracle become ordinary. When you started that new job, you were so excited. You told all your friends. You knew it was God's favor. Don't lose the excitement just because you've had it for five years.

When you fell in love after meeting the person of your dreams, you knew it was the result of God's goodness. Don't take it for granted. Remember what God has done.

We worked and prayed for three years to acquire the former Houston Rockets basketball arena for our church. When the city leaders approved our purchase, we celebrated a dream come true. Nearly ten years later, the building could become common and ordinary. But I have to admit that every time I walk in the building, I can't help but say, "God, thank You. You have done more than I can ask or think."

Don't let what was once a miracle become so common that it's ordinary.

TODAY'S PRAYER

Father, thank You that You have placed seeds of greatness in me. I have recounted Your goodness in my life, the amazing things You have done, and I believe that You are breathing new life into me at this very moment. I am fanning the flames and stirring up my gift, and I believe You are restoring my passion. Amen.

TODAY'S THOUGHT

We need to stir ourselves up, to replenish our supply of God's good gifts on a daily basis. Like the Israeli people in the wilderness who had to gather God's miraculous provisions of manna afresh each morning, we, too, cannot get by on yesterday's supply. We need fresh enthusiasm each day. Our lives need to be inspired, infused, and filled afresh with God's goodness every day.

Live in Amazement

Scripture Reading: 2 Corinthians 3

But we all, with unveiled face, beholding as in a mirror the glory of the Lord, are being transformed into the same image from glory to glory, just as by the Spirit of the Lord.
2 Corinthians 3:18 NKJV

We all have seen God's hand of favor in some way—an opened a door, a promotion, protection on the freeway, meeting someone who has been a blessing. In my own life, when I look at my children, I think, "God, You're amazing." When I see Victoria, I think, "God, You've been good to me." Driving up to my house, I think, "Lord, thank You for Your favor." It is so important to live in amazement at what God has done.

I read about a famous surgeon who so loved medicine that he continued to go to work every day even into his late eighties. He had invented a certain procedure that he had performed over ten thousand times. When he was asked if he ever grew tired of performing his procedure, he said, "No, because I act like every operation is my very first one." He was saying, "I don't let it become so ordinary that I lose the awe."

What has God done for you? Do you have healthy children? Do you have people to love? Do you have a place to work? Do you realize your gifts and talents come from God? Do you recognize what seemed like a lucky break was God directing your steps?

There are miracles all around us. Don't take them for

granted. Don't lose the amazement of God's works. Sometimes we hold back, thinking we'll get excited when the next best thing comes along. Only then will we allow that spring back in our step. But I've learned if you aren't happy where you are, you won't get where you want to be.

You need to sow a seed. Maybe nothing exciting is going on; perhaps you're facing big challenges. You could easily grow discouraged and give up on your dreams. But you are sowing a seed when you go to work with a smile, give it your best, offer kindness to others, and show gratitude for what you have.

God will take that seed and grow it to bring something exciting into your life. The Scripture tells us God will take us from glory to glory and from victory to victory. You may be in between victories right now, but keep your passion and hold on to your enthusiasm. The good news is another victory is on its way!

TODAY'S PRAYER

Father, You are the Creator of the universe, and I believe You are breathing Your life into me. You have opened doors, given promotions and protections, and worked in so many amazing ways in my life. I believe that You are working right now to lift me to another level of favor. Amen.

TODAY'S THOUGHT

On the way to our victories we will always face the weariness test. The key is to not be discouraged about your past or present while you are in the process of being taken from glory to glory and victory to victory. Stand strong and hold on to your enthusiasm.

Put Your Heart into It

Scripture Reading: 2 Thessalonians 3

*For you yourselves know how you ought to follow our example.
. . . we worked night and day, laboring and toiling so that we
would not be a burden to any of you.*

2 Thessalonians 3:7–8

Ecclesiastes says, "Whatever you do, do it with all your heart and you are honoring God." When you give 100 percent effort, you do it to the best of your ability; because you're honoring God, you will have His blessing. That means it will go better. It will be easier, and you will accomplish more.

Let's make it practical. When you do the dishes, don't complain; do it with all your heart and you honor God. When you mow the lawn, don't drag around all sour. Mow it with enthusiasm. Mow it like you're on a mission from God. With every step, thank God that your legs work. Thank God that you're healthy. At the office, don't give it a halfhearted effort. Don't just do what is required to get by. You're not working unto people. You're working unto God. Do it with all your heart. Do it with a smile. Give it your very best.

When I was growing up, there was a police officer who directed traffic at the Galleria Mall in Houston. His assignment was to keep people safe on one of the busiest intersections in the city. Traffic could be backed up for five or ten minutes. He didn't just direct traffic like normal, he practically danced while he directed.

Both hands would be constantly moving. He had that whistle and he held his head like a drum major. His feet would dance here and there. He could direct traffic and moonwalk at the same time. He really put on a show. Drivers pulled over just to watch him. He did not drag through the day. He didn't feel bad about going to work. He was passionate.

That's the way you should be. Don't drag through the day. Don't get stuck in a rut. Whatever you do, put your heart into it. Put a spring in your step. Wear a smile on your face. You honor God when you do it with all your heart.

TODAY'S PRAYER

Father, thank You that because Your joy is my strength,
I can enjoy my life to the fullest today and do everything I do
with all of my heart. I want to live this day to give You
pleasure and honor. Fill me with the Holy Spirit
and renew my spirit today. Amen.

TODAY'S THOUGHT

In the midst of the ordinary, you can choose to have
an extraordinary attitude toward your work. The Scripture
tells us to do everything we do with our whole hearts, "to
never lag in zeal" (Romans 12:11 AMP). Make a decision that
you are not going to live another day without the joy of the
Lord in your life; without love, peace, and passion;
without being excited about your life.

Be the Best That You Can Be

Scripture Reading: Ecclesiastes 5

Moreover, when God gives someone wealth and possessions, and the ability to enjoy them, to accept their lot and be happy in their toil—this is a gift of God. They seldom reflect on the days of their life, because God keeps them occupied with gladness of heart.

Ecclesiastes 5:19–20

The Scripture says God has given us the power to enjoy what's allotted to us, which means I don't have the power to enjoy your life. You may have more money, more gifts, more friends, and a better job. But if you put me in your life, I will not enjoy it.

You are uniquely created to run your own race. Quit wishing you were someone else or thinking things such as, "If I had his talent . . ." If God wanted you to have his talent, He would give it to you. Take what you have and develop it. Make the most of your gifts.

Instead of thinking things such as, "If I had her looks . . . ," be grateful for the looks God gave you. That's not an accident. The life you have is perfectly matched for you.

So many people try to be something they are not. I've known dark-skinned people who apply cream to try to be lighter and light-skinned people who go to a tanning bed to try to be darker. I had an older lady touch my hair at a book signing recently. She said, "Joel, I wish I had that curly hair," even though her hair looked fine.

Why don't you get excited about your life? Be excited about your looks, your talent, and your personality. When you are passionate about who you are, you bring honor to God. That's when God will breathe in your direction, and the seeds of greatness He's planted on the inside will spring forth.

Really, it's an insult to God to wish you were someone else. You are saying, "God, why did You make me subpar?" God didn't make anyone inferior or second-class. You are a masterpiece, fully loaded and totally equipped for the race that's designed for you.

Your attitude should be: "I may not be as tall or as talented as someone else, but that's okay. Nobody will ever be a better me. I'm anointed to be me. I'm equipped to be me. And not only that, it's also easy to be me." It's easy to be yourself. It's easy to run your race, because you're fully equipped for what you need.

TODAY'S PRAYER

Father, thank You that I can be passionate and excited about who I am because You created me to be Your masterpiece. Thank You for fully equipping me to run my own race with the looks and the talents and gifts I have. Help me to make the most of my gifts for Your glory. Amen.

TODAY'S THOUGHT

Before you were ever formed in your mother's womb, God saw you. And the Scripture teaches that God has already approved and accepted you. He may not be pleased with every decision you have made, but understand this extremely important truth: God is pleased with you. If God approves you, why don't you approve yourself?

Keep Working and Growing

Scripture Reading: Psalm 92

The righteous will flourish like a palm tree, they
will grow like a cedar of Lebanon; planted in the house of the
LORD, they will flourish in the courts of our God. They will still
bear fruit in old age, they will stay fresh and green . . .

Psalm 92:12–14

If you want to stay passionate, you have to stay productive. You have to have a reason to get out of bed in the morning. When you're not producing, you're not growing. When you quit being productive, you start slowly dying. You may retire from your job, but don't ever retire from life. Stay busy. Keep using your mind. Keep helping others. Volunteer at the hospital. Babysit your relatives' children. Mentor a young person.

God promises if you keep Him in first place, He will give you a long, satisfied life. How long is a long life? Until you are satisfied. If you quit producing at fifty and you're satisfied, the promise is fulfilled.

I don't know about you, but I've got too much in me to die right now. I'm not satisfied. I have dreams that have yet to be realized. I have messages that I've yet to give. I have children to enjoy. When I get to be about ninety, and I'm still strong and full of joy, I'll say, "Okay, God, I'm satisfied. I'm ready for my change of address. Let's go."

Some people quit living at fifty, but we don't bury them until they are eighty. Even though they've been alive, they haven't been really living. Maybe they went through disappointments.

They had some failures, or somebody did them wrong, and they lost their joy. They just settled and stopped enjoying life.

But God has another victory in your future. You wouldn't be breathing if God didn't have something great in front of you. You need to get back your passion. God is not finished with you. God will complete what He started in your life. The Scripture says God will bring us to a flourishing finish—not a fizzling finish. Shake off the self-pity, shake off what didn't work out. You may have a reason to feel sorry for yourself, but you don't have a right. God said He will take what was meant for your harm and not only bring you out, but also bring you out better off than you were before.

TODAY'S PRAYER

Father, thank You for the promise that You will bring my life to a flourishing finish no matter what I'm experiencing today. You can make the rest of my life the best of my life. Something great is still in front of me. I believe You have an "after this" in my future. Amen.

TODAY'S THOUGHT

You can't let the hurt, the pain, or the bad break cause you to sit back in self-pity and lose your passion. Shake off what didn't work out. Quit mourning over what you've lost. A full life is still in front of you. You have not danced your best dance. You have not laughed your best laugh. You have not dreamed your best dream. God will always have an "after this" for you.

Get in Agreement with God

Scripture Reading: Psalm 24

Lift up your heads, you gates; lift them up, you ancient doors, that the King of glory may come in. Who is he, this King of glory? The LORD Almighty—he is the King of glory.

Psalm 24:9–10

David said, "Lift up your head, and the King of glory will come in." As long as your head is down and you are discouraged, with no joy, no passion, and no zeal, the King of glory will not come. Instead, get up in the morning and say, "Father, I'm excited about this day." When you're really alive, hopeful, grateful, passionate, and productive, the King of glory, the Most High God, will come in and make a way where there is no way.

I know a popular minister who led his church for many years and was such a great speaker he was in constant demand. But he was diagnosed with Parkinson's disease and eventually lost the ability to speak. He had to resign from his church. He once was so eloquent, strong, and vibrant, but just when things looked as if his career was over and his best days were behind him, he sent me a manuscript with a note: "Joel, I can't speak anymore, so I've taken up writing. Here's a look at my newest book."

We all have unfair things happen. Don't let it sour your life. Just because you had a bad break or you can't do what you used to do doesn't mean you're supposed to sit on the sidelines. If you can't speak, write. If you can't run, walk. If you can't stand up, just sit up. Do whatever you can do. As long as you have breath, don't lose your passion.

Think about the apostle Paul: He was thrown in prison at the peak of his career. Just when it was all coming together he had this major disappointment. Paul could have become depressed and thought, "Too bad for me." Instead, he kept his passion, and while in prison, he wrote more than half of the New Testament. What looked like a setback was really a setup for God to do something greater in Paul's life.

You may have been through some bad breaks and unfair situations. Stay passionate. God is still on the throne. If you keep your head up, the King of glory will still come in and guide you to where He wants you to be.

TODAY'S PRAYER

Father God, You are the amazing King of glory,
the Most High God, and You are the keeper of my dreams.
There is no power greater than Yours. I believe that You order
my steps and my stops. So I'm keeping my passion up and
moving forward in faith, knowing that You have
something greater in store. Amen.

TODAY'S THOUGHT

You may be discouraged because your plans have not worked out, but stay passionate. God is directing your steps even if it looks like a setback. God has something better in store. Thank God for your difficulties just as much as for your open doors. I believe and declare you will see the exceeding, abundant, above-and-beyond future that God has in store.

Look Ahead

Scripture Reading: Isaiah 43

For I am about to do something new. See, I have already begun!
Do you not see it? I will make a pathway through the
wilderness. I will create rivers in the dry wasteland.

Isaiah 43:19 NLT

It's tempting to go through life looking in the rearview mirror. When you are always looking back, you become focused on what didn't work out, on who hurt you, and on the mistakes you've made, such as, "If only I would have finished college." "If only I'd spent more time with my children." "If only I'd been raised in a better environment."

As long as you're living in regret, focused on the negative things of the past, you won't move ahead to the bright future God has in store. You need to let go of what didn't work out. Let go of your hurts and pains. Let go of your mistakes and failures.

If you keep bringing the negative baggage from yesterday into today, your future will be poisoned. You can't change or do anything about the past, but you can do something about right now. You may have had an unfair past, but you don't have to have an unfair future. You may have had a rough start, but it's not how you start, it's how you finish.

Don't let a hurtful relationship sour your life. Don't let a bad break, a betrayal, a divorce, or a bad childhood cause you to settle for less in life. Move forward and God will pay you back. Move forward and God will vindicate you. Move forward and you'll come into a new beginning. Nothing that's happened to you is a surprise to God. The loss of a loved one didn't catch God off guard. God's plan for your life did not end just because your business didn't make it, or a relationship failed, or you had a difficult child.

Here's the question: Will you become stuck and bitter or will you shake it off and move forward, knowing your best days are still ahead?

The next time you are in your car, notice that there's a big windshield in the front and a very small rearview mirror. The reason the front windshield is so big and the rearview mirror is so small is that what's happened in the past is not nearly as important as what is in your future. Where you're going is a lot more important than where you've been.

TODAY'S PRAYER

Father God, thank You that nothing that happens to me ever catches You off guard. I'm excited about this day. I need to let go of past regrets, hurts, and pains that I can't do anything about today. This is it. I'm letting go of the past and moving forward with my life. I believe that You will vindicate me with new beginnings and that my best days are still ahead. Amen.

TODAY'S THOUGHT

We can't do anything about the past, and we have no guarantees regarding the future; we can only do something about right now. The good news is, your past does not have to poison your future. God still has good things in store for you. If you bring it all to Jesus and let it go, today can be a new beginning.

Ditch the Baggage

Scripture Reading: Ruth 1

This is what the LORD says: "Restrain your voice from weeping and your eyes from tears, for your work will be rewarded," declares the LORD. "They will return from the land of the enemy. So there is hope for your descendants," declares the LORD.

Jeremiah 31:16–17

If you stay focused on the past, you'll get stuck where you are. That's the reason some people don't have any joy. They've lost their enthusiasm. They're dragging around all this baggage from the past. Someone offended them, and they have that stuffed in their resentment bags. They lost their tempers or said some things they shouldn't have, which they've tucked in their bags of guilt and condemnation. Ten years ago their loved one died, and their hurt and pain is packed in their disappointment bag. Growing up they weren't treated right—there's another suitcase full of bitterness. They've got their regret bags, containing all the things they wish they'd done differently.

Life is too short to live that way. Learn to travel light. Every morning when you get up, forgive those who hurt you. Forgive your spouse for what was said. Forgive your boss for being rude. Forgive yourself for mistakes you've made. Let go of the setbacks and the disappointments from yesterday. Start every morning afresh and anew. God did not create you to carry around all that baggage. You may have been holding on to it for years. It's not going to change until you do something about it. Put your foot down and say, "That's it. I'm not living in regrets and disappointments. I'm not dwelling on relationships that didn't work out. I'm letting go of the past and moving forward with my life."

You should focus on what you can change, not what you cannot change. What's done is done. If somebody offended, mistreated, or disappointed you, the hurts can't be undone. You can get bitter or you can forgive those who hurt you and go on.

No matter what happens, big or small, if you make the choice to let it go and move forward, you won't let the past poison your future. You may have had some bad breaks, but that didn't stop God's plan for your life. He still has amazing things in your future.

TODAY'S PRAYER

Father, You know every hardship and hurt, every unfair and difficult situation I have faced and will ever face. I choose to let go of the things that are holding me back from the fantastic future You have for me. I choose to forgive others as You have forgiven me, and I ask You to cleanse me from any bitterness. I believe You are moving me forward with Your plan for my life. Amen.

TODAY'S THOUGHT

When one door closes, stay in faith and God will open another door. If a dream dies, move forward and dream another dream. Your life is not over because you lost a loved one, went through a divorce, lost a job, or didn't get the house you wanted. You would not be alive unless God had another victory in front of you.

Get Ready for New Things

Then he said to me, "Speak a prophetic message to these bones and say, 'Dry bones, listen to the word of the LORD! This is what the Sovereign LORD says: Look! I am going to put breath into you and make you live again! . . . I am the LORD.'"
Ezekiel 37:4–6 NLT

Pastor Dutch Sheets told a story about a forty-year-old lady having open-heart bypass surgery for a blocked artery. Although this is a delicate procedure, it's considered a routine surgery and performed successfully more than 230,000 times every year. During the operation, the surgeon clamped off the main vein flowing to the heart and hooked it to a machine that pumps the blood and keeps the lungs working. The heart actually stops beating while the vein is being bypassed. When the procedure is over and the machine is removed, the warmth from the body's blood normally causes the heart to start beating again. If that doesn't work, they have drugs that will wake up the heart.

This lady was on the operating table and the bypass was finished, so they let her blood start flowing, but her heart did not start beating. They then gave her the usual drugs with no success. She had no heartbeat. The surgeon massaged her heart with his hand to stimulate that muscle and get it beating again, but even that did not work. He was so troubled. It looked as if his patient was finished. Then he whispered in her ear, "Mary, I've done everything I can do. Now I need you to tell your heart to beat again." He stepped back and heard *bump, bump, bump*. Her heart kicked in and started beating.

Do you need to tell your heart to beat again? Maybe life didn't turn out like you had hoped. Now you're just sitting on the sideline. You've got to get your passion back. Get your fire back. Tell your heart to dream again. Tell your heart to love again. Tell your heart to laugh again. Tell your heart to believe again.

The Most High God breathed His life into you. You've got what it takes. This is your time. This is your moment. Shake off fear and insecurity and get ready for favor, get ready for increase, get ready for the fullness of your destiny. You can, you will!

TODAY'S PRAYER

Father, thank You that You give me the power to speak to my heart and get back whatever good things I may have left behind in the past. You are breathing Your life into me and making me alive again. I am ready for Your goodness and Your favor. I believe that I will see increase and the fullness of the destiny You created for me. Amen.

TODAY'S THOUGHT

You may have suffered a setback, but don't sit around in self-pity. Tell your heart to beat again. Tell your heart to love again. Someone may have done you wrong, but don't let it poison you. Tell your heart to forgive again. Maybe a dream didn't work out, but nothing will change if you just expect more of the same. Tell your heart to dream again.

DAY 11

Give Life All You've Got

Scripture Reading: Isaiah 55

"So you'll go out in joy, you'll be led into a whole and complete life. The mountains and hills will lead the parade, bursting with song. All the trees of the forest will join the procession, exuberant with applause. No more thistles, but giant sequoias, no more thornbushes, but stately pines—monuments to me, to God . . ."
Isaiah 55:12–13 MSG

I have a friend who went through a divorce after twenty-six years of marriage. His wife left him a note saying she'd found someone else. He was an outgoing, fun, and energetic person, but after she left him, he was solemn, discouraged, and he had no joy, no life.

I told him what I'm telling you: "This is not the end. God has a new beginning. But you've got to do your part and tell your heart to beat again." Little by little, he recovered his joy, his vision, and his passion. Then God brought a beautiful lady into his life and they married. He told me a while back that he's happier than he's ever been.

You may have let the pressures of life weigh you down, and you're all solemn and serious. You need to tell your heart to laugh again. Get back your joy and enthusiasm.

Jesus said in Revelation 2, "I have one thing against you: You have left your first love." He didn't say you've lost your love; He says you've left your first love. That means you can go get it. You haven't lost your passion. You just left it. Go get it.

You haven't lost the love for your family; you've just left it—now go get it. You haven't lost that dream; it's still there in you. You just left it. You have to go get it.

You may have had some setbacks, but this is a new day. Stir up what God put on the inside. Fan the flame. Don't be just barely alive. God wants you to be really alive. Dreams are coming back to life. Your vision is being renewed. Your passion is being restored. Hearts are beating again. Get ready for God's goodness and favor.

You can live a life of victory. You can overcome every obstacle. You can accomplish your dreams. You can set new levels for your family. Not only are you able, but I also declare you will become all God created you to be. Winning is in your DNA. You will live a blessed, rewarding life. My encouragement is: Don't settle where you are.

TODAY'S PRAYER

Father, thank You that this is a new day and my dreams and vision and passions are being renewed by the power of Your Holy Spirit. I believe that I will rise to new levels and become all You created me to be. I will not settle for anything less. Amen.

TODAY'S THOUGHT

You have seeds of greatness on the inside. Put these principles into action each day. Get up in the morning expecting good things, go through the day positive, focused on your vision, running your race, knowing that you are well able. You can, you will!

STAY**CONNECTED,**
BE**BLESSED.**

From thoughtful articles to powerful blogs, podcasts and more, JoelOsteen.com is full of inspirations that will give you encouragement and confidence in your daily life.

AVAILABLE ON JOELOSTEEN.COM

This daily devotional from Joel and Victoria will help you grow in your relationship with the Lord and equip you to be everything God intends you to be.

**STREAMING**

Miss a broadcast? Watch Joel Osteen on demand, and see Joel LIVE on Sundays.

PODCAST

The podcast is a great way to listen to Joel where you want, when you want.

CONNECT WITH US

Join our community of believers on your favorite social network.

PUT JOEL IN YOUR POCKET

Get the inspiration and encouragement of Joel Osteen on your iPhone, iPad or Android device! Our app puts Joel's messages, devotions and more at your fingertips.

Thanks for helping us make a difference in the lives of millions around the world.

Notes

Notes

Notes